Jess Phillips was first elected as the Labour [MP] [for] Birmingham Yardley in 2015 and was elected [Chair of] the Women's Parliamentary Labour Party in S[eptember] 2016. Before becoming an MP, she worked with v[ictims of] domestic violence, sexual violence and human tr[afficking,] and she continues to speak up on behalf of those wh[o struggle] to have their voice heard. Jess lives with her husban[d and two] sons in Birmingham, where she was born and rais[ed.]

Praise for other titles by Jess Phillips

Everywoman: One Woman's Truth About Speaking the Truth

'Jess Phillips writes like she talks: brilliantly. Her humour and passion shine through every page. Loved it.'
Robert Webb

'Joyfully candid and very funny.'
Guardian

'Jess Phillips knows the truth . . . and here she shows how scary and sad as well as joyful and liberating the answers can be.'
Damian Barr

'Lord knows we need more MPs like Jess Phillips . . . As fresh as mountain air amid the Westminster tumbleweed.'
Metro

'A narrative that is by turns witty and furious.'
Gabby Hinsliff, *Guardian* **Best Political Books of the Year**

'Arresting.'
Observer

*Truth to Power: How to Call Time on Bullsh*t, Speak Up &
Make a Difference*

'Someone like Jess Phillips in politics does a powerful thing.
It makes millions of women like her think, "If she can do
politics, maybe I could do politics too."'
Caitlin Moran

'There's nobody else at Westminster quite like Jess Phillips.
She is fearless and funny, riotous and rebellious, maverick
and mischievous.'
The Times

'Will ruffle some feathers.'
Stylist

THE LIFE OF AN MP

JESS PHILLIPS

GALLERY BOOKS UK

First published in Great Britain by Gallery Books,
an imprint of Simon & Schuster UK Ltd, as *Everything You
Really Need to Know About Politics: My Life as an MP,* 2021

This edition published in Great Britain by Gallery Books,
an imprint of Simon & Schuster UK Ltd, 2022

3 5 7 9 10 8 6 4

Simon & Schuster UK Ltd
1st Floor
222 Gray's Inn Road
London WC1X 8HB

www.simonandschuster.co.uk
www.simonandschuster.com.au
www.simonandschuster.co.in

Simon & Schuster Australia, Sydney
Simon & Schuster India, New Delhi

A CIP catalogue record for this book is available from the British Library

Paperback ISBN: 978-1-3985-0092-1
eBook ISBN: 978-1-3985-0091-4

Typeset in Bembo by M Rules
Printed in the UK by CPI Group (UK) Ltd, Croydon, CR0 4YY

MIX
Paper from
responsible sources
FSC® C171272

For Luke Trainor and his family, Leila, Gabriel and Kane

Contents

Introduction

Welcome to Parliament, the Place is Falling Apart

'You can't park in the underground car park today, ma'am, there's some sort of an alarm going off down there.' There was a definite air of nonchalance in the voice of the security guard as he checked my pass at the barrier to the Palace of Westminster on an unremarkable day at work.

'What's happened?' I asked, alert to the fact that security threats in Parliament are not unusual and can be dangerous.

'Oh nothing serious,' he shrugged, 'just something to do with carbon monoxide poisoning.'

Oh, well that's all right then. Angry activists have not breached the walls, armed political dissidents are not roaming the corridors – it's just a light poison alert in the airless place I have been parking my car all week.

Later that day, I received a text message that read, 'Unfortunately, owing to failing masonry Black Rod's Garden Entrance and St Stephen's Entrance have had to close. There are also issues with the scaffolding at Cromwell Green Entrance and this will also be closing soon.' If the deadly poison doesn't get you, chances are an ancient gargoyle could fall on your head at any moment.

Welcome to Parliament. The place is falling apart.

However, the bar is set high here – terrorism, war, global pandemics, death threats, mass unemployment – and so risks that would condemn any other place of work pass without even the slightest eyebrow raise. At times, Westminster is less a palace of legislation and more like a real-life simulation of Bowser's castles in *Super Mario*. Luckily, I spent the entire summer holiday of 1992 smashing *Super Mario Bros 3* on the original Nintendo at my mate Bryony's house. If only crushing the big boss in Parliament was as simple as jumping on his head three times. Bowser was an easy foe to slay in comparison to the years of ingrained privilege and entitlement that currently grip the politics of our country. A pair of Italian plumbers would have very little chance of smashing it and as for Princess Peach, she would fare as well in Westminster as she does in the game.

The onus is on all of us to change the rules of the game and I believe we can. But first of all, it would help if that decrepit palace were opened up, if the inner workings of our politics were demystified and if we could poke some much-needed holes in the barriers that keep people feeling that Westminster and its inhabitants are nothing like them. People like you and I have every right to walk the corridors of Westminster. In fact, I would argue that we are the people who have the greatest right to be working in Westminster: those of us who send our children to state schools, who get our healthcare exclusively from the NHS, who are more likely to work in the public sector, rely on public parks for recreation, travel on a bus or end up on the front line in a war. Politicians routinely make decisions that directly affect the lives of single mothers who rely on subsidised childcare, for example, but very few single mothers see that as a reason why more of them should be in

Westminster making those decisions. We as citizens should not have stuff done to us by people who have convinced us that their funny terminology and fancy buildings don't suit us.

I often see groups of school children and tourists from all over the world walking around the areas of the Palace of Westminster. They look awestruck. A building so steeped in history, so palatial in its size and sense of duty, it crushes you. When I first started working there, I would always choose routes across the estate that took me through the most magnificent expanses and I used to get neck ache from gawping up at the splendour. If I'd known then what I know now, I would have been looking out for falling masonry. I do love the place, really love it, and I feel a sense of pride in being able to scuttle around this grand, labyrinthine institution. I want people to be amazed and inspired by all of the history, I just don't want anyone to be crushed or excluded by its pomposity – because as well as being beautiful and grand, it is also just my office, and I want everyone to feel as if it is theirs, too.

I am often asked why I got involved in politics. To be completely honest, I don't really have a definitive answer; the truth lies somewhere in between the different versions of the story that I tell each time I am asked. They are as follows:

1. I wanted to change the world. This is undoubtedly true but it makes me sound a bit like a contestant in Miss World. We have all become very cynical about the idea that politicians actually do the job in order to improve things and that is a real shame. I would say that 90 per cent of MPs genuinely want to make the world a better place (yes, even the one

you absolutely despise and don't agree with at all),*
it's just that we all have a different idea of how to
achieve this. For example, I don't think that starv-
ing children through withdrawing family benefits
encourages people to go to work and 'help themselves'. Just because someone took away your benefits
doesn't mean there is suddenly a cushy job waiting
for you, one that you are qualified for, that you can
get to and that works around your childcare. Many of
my Conservative colleagues do think that and it's not
because they hate the poor – they genuinely think
that being tougher on low-income families will help
them. Changing the world for the better looks different to everyone but it is what most politicians do
want to achieve. Some are just really shit at it.

2. I saw that decisions were being made by people who
knew naff all about the lives of the people I was
working with at Black Country Women's Aid, so I
thought I'd better become one of the people who
made the decisions. It is commonly said in politics,
'It's nothing personal, it's just politics.' Well that,
my friend, is utter bullshit. Yes, politics is rough and
tumble; yes, you have to grow a thick skin – but the

---

* 10 per cent definitely don't give a toss about the world but played toy soldiers as children and have a perverse sense of how bloody exceptional they
are and, quite frankly, are convinced that they were born to rule. I imagine
that their parents held them aloft on the edge of a great canyon and said,
'One day, my little prince, all this will be yours.' There has never been a
better example of this than Alexander Boris de Pfeffel Johnson. Who, had he
been called Carl Thompson and grown up in a 1930s semi in Wigan, would
not have got where he has. Make no mistake, he doesn't want to change the
world, he just wants to rule it so he might one day get a statue.

idea that it is not personal is only ever espoused by people who have never needed political decisions to change their lives. Tell it to people living in bombed-out Aleppo who have lost their loved ones and their home. 'Soz guys, nothing personal!' When hardworking single mothers hear politicians spouting on about how children from single-parent families are lower achievers, it probably feels pretty personal. Politics is personal. It was personal to the women who lived in the refuge where I worked, to those who watched the defunding of the children's rape counselling services and to those who couldn't get a place in a refuge so were left living in fear. It certainly felt very personal to me and so I decided to take it on. Personally.

3. I have always been involved in politics. I was raised under Thatcher's government by socialist activist parents and grandparents. I was holding a banner before I could feed myself and I suspect that in certain lights you can still see the 'Ban the Bomb' face paint that was scrawled on my face on a daily basis as a child before I was squeezed into a buggy intended for two children but always accommodating at least four and pushed around some march or another. Westminster might have seemed inaccessible but politics never did. Politics is ours – yours and mine – and I will spend my life trying to make you, reader, feel as involved as my mom and dad made me feel when they dragged me and my siblings round our city and country fighting political injustice – although maybe with fewer lollipops to bribe you. Politics is ours.

4. I wanted a career in politics. Shock horror! A person wanted to make a living from the thing she was interested in. It is not okay in modern Britain to say that you wanted to have a good career and so you got involved in politics. Jokers like Nigel Farage (who, as far as I can tell, has been involved in politics far more than any other line of work, was a politician for decades and makes a shed load of cash from being political) like to make out that the worst bogeyman in politics is the 'Career Politician'. Well, being a politician is my career and I want to progress at it (I know, I know – outrageous, isn't it?). I also want to be paid for doing my job – like most people in the country. Lots of people, me included, spend a lot of time volunteering and helping others out of the goodness of their hearts but, let's face it, this is only sustainable as a career for the independently wealthy. I remember a Tory woman once saying to me that she had taken a huge pay cut to become an MP and that she couldn't have done it had her husband not become a senior partner in a law firm. To which I replied that my income had more than doubled when I became an MP, that I was the family breadwinner and that actually, I felt pretty wealthy. No word of a lie, she then said, 'Gosh, well, we couldn't afford the children's schooling if I were the breadwinner.' I told her that boarding school was not compulsory but I don't think she could quite compute what I was saying. Mind you, another Tory woman once said to me while drunk, on hearing that I lived in

Birmingham, 'The place is disgusting and I would rather die than have to live there.' Which is really polite. Turns out they don't teach manners in those fancy schools. Anyway, I digress. For me, being a politician was a solid career move from working in the voluntary sector at Black Country Women's Aid. It was a step up the ladder in both influence and finances and more people should admit that. Otherwise it's like being a Miss World contestant pretending that it is world peace that primarily led you to the pageant rather than wanting to be considered the hottest woman in the world. In other words, it's okay to want to make a good and respectable living out of politics – or to want to be the hottest woman on the patriarchal planet.*

I am still not entirely sure which of the above factors was the one that gave me the final shove to step up and serve. I am afraid I don't remember the moment that I decided that the fancy awe-inspiring Palace of Westminster was for me. I do remember talking about it with my family, friends and colleagues for a while, but it seemed more like a joke, or even a

---

* Obviously, I think that Miss World is awful and sexist and a disgusting reduction of womanhood as seen through the eyes of creepy men, but the guilty feminist in me does get why you might want a massive tiara to show what a hottie you are. My guiltiest moment in Parliament as a feminist was following a debate about abortion in Northern Ireland, where we were fighting for the rights of women to have freedom over their own bodies. I read out accounts of Irish women who had had to travel to my hometown in mainland UK in order to get an abortion and it was an honour to give voice to their struggle. Afterwards, when I watched the video of the speech, all I could think was that my hair looked a mess and I wished I'd dry shampooed my fringe before I went into the Commons chamber. Patriarchy is a bitch.

threat – 'Well! Maybe I'll run for Parliament and show them.' Until it wasn't a joke and it was something I was doing.

I vividly remember when the regional director of the West Midlands Labour Party called one Saturday morning to tell me that the selections for various local seats would be happening soon and asked if I would consider putting myself forward as a possible candidate. While he was still on the phone, I shouted downstairs to my husband, Tom, 'Tooooommmmm. They are asking if I want to have a go at running for Parliament, what do you think?' His response was something along the lines of, 'Yeah, seems like a fair plan.' I bet he didn't take his eyes of the telly while agreeing to one of the most life-changing decisions we would ever make. If anything, he sounded perplexed as to why I was even asking him in the first place. I returned to the call and said, 'All right, then.'

There was no massive family conference; we didn't think about the logistics of our life being smashed beyond recognition or how the hell we would manage with an eight-year-old and a four-year-old if I had to live away. To be honest, when I look back, I cannot believe how little we considered it all. Perhaps it was our ignorance of how things worked that allowed us to dare to be so cavalier. It is also only now that I realise how rare it is for a fairly young charity worker and a lift engineer with two small kids to feel as if politics was something that belonged firmly to us.

I am asked a lot, 'Is the job what you expected?' The answer to this is simple: when I arrived in Westminster, I had absolutely no expectations at all. I knew that there were laws I wanted to change (Northern Ireland abortion laws – tick) and people I wanted to provide better services for (victims of domestic and sexual abuse – partial tick), but I had no preconceptions about what the day-to-day would entail, nor what the place was like, how it breathed and who wound the organs. I had only been in the building two or three times when I was elected to work there for the foreseeable future. I was passionate about feminism, rights and justice, for sure (you don't grow up with socialist parents like mine without being a hopeless idealist), but I had no particular sense of mission or clear plan for the future. I just wanted to be a worker ant in the halls of change.

It took only a matter of weeks for all of that to shift and for me to build a very clear idea of what my purpose in that place was. And that is the very reason that I am writing this book. After I was elected, my mission became to make politics for everyone, to make Westminster accessible for people like you and me. We built that building, staffed it and made sure it housed one of the best democracies in the world, and yet we are so often mystified by it because it looks like Hogwarts and people there wear necklaces that belong to the actual crown jewels.

I want to write about what it is *actually* like to be a member of Parliament – what my days are like, what the differences are between my life in London and my life in the constituency. I find that when my place of work is dramatised in books or on TV, they usually miss the parts of the place that make it great. Dramatisations are often about war – Churchill gets a lot of reel time – or they are about affairs and deceit, as if behind every curtain is someone plotting the downfall of their political nemesis or a Secretary of State with their skirt hitched up revealing their stockings, mid-tryst with a bodyguard. (Someone should work up a crossover and make a sexy Second World War film with Churchill in stockings in a cupboard. Churchill never gets any steamy scenes.)

In every movie that features Parliament, there is at least one scene where someone makes the most heart-stoppingly brilliant speech. In my experience, movie-worthy speeches in Parliament are as rare as hens' teeth and I have only ever seen a handful. Believe me, if you think you don't belong in Parliament or in political life because you have never made a rousing speech or are crap at public speaking then you are wrong – you would be in good company in politics.

My favourite onscreen rendition of Parliament is that bit in Hollywood disaster movies where obviously all the action happens in America but in order to show that the aliens/meteor/tidal wave is a global problem they do a quick montage of the disaster hitting famous sites around the world. Along with the Great Wall of China, the Taj Mahal and the Sydney Opera House, the Houses of Parliament are often exploded to smithereens. At which point my kids always say, 'You just died, Mom, sorry.'

As for the way things are reported by the press (who obviously work in Parliament too), the dullest of meetings can end up sounding as if they were tense, exciting or full of intrigue. I know I am not really selling what you are about to read, as it might seem as if I am saying political life is boring – which of course it is sometimes. But what I am really saying is that the bits that make my job brilliant, heart-warming, heart-breaking and exciting are very rarely talked about or depicted. No wonder it is so easy for people to look at political life and assume that it is inaccessible, lofty or exclusive. It can indeed be all of those things, but only if we let it. So let's talk about the realities of political life and the effect it has on the lives of all of us.

Every day, people write to me and say things like, 'I am sorry to bother you, I have never written to an MP before,' as if I am in a different category to them or they are going above their station. Too many people think that all politicians are morally bankrupt gold diggers who spend all their time on yachts with newspaper editors and tech lobbyists – because that is the stuff that makes the headlines. No wonder we are one of the most hated professions in the country. A woman in my local Greggs once said to me while serving me a steak bake, 'I guess I, the taxpayer, am paying for this steak bake.' I am afraid to tell you, dear reader, that parliamentary expenses do not cover my steak bakes. The only taxpayer who funds my steak bakes is me.*

I am not saying this in order to defend MPs – far from it, some of them are absolute rob dogs. I am saying it because when we start to believe that politics is a game played by rich toffs and crooked corrupt pigs then we start to opt out of the system. And when we do that, we hand it to them on a plate. The toffs and the crooks love it when ordinary people look at the political landscape and think, 'Let them carry on in their big palace thinking they are better than us.' They love it

---

* Other bakes are available from other outlets. But let's face it, you cannot beat a Greggs steak bake. When the Greggs opened at Westminster station, it was genuinely more of an event for those in Parliament than the Queen's speech at the opening of Parliament. A Westminster office is now considered incomplete without a half-eaten pack of yum yums in it.

when, come election day, someone thinks, 'What's the point in going out in the rain to vote, it won't change anything.' Today, as I write, I am genuinely worried about the small entitled cabal of men who gallivanted around the country declaring that we must 'Take Back Control' as if they were doing the country a solid favour. They weren't. What they meant was that *they* wanted all the control. You are letting them off the hook every time you decide politics doesn't affect you or that you can't affect politics. Don't let the arseholes off the hook.

This book is here to take you inside the daily realities of Westminster. I don't mean that it's going to bore you to death with a blow-by-blow account of what it's like to sit on the Statutory Instrument Debate on Naval regulations 1968–2020, rather I want to demystify the places and practice of politics so that we can all start to own it again. I want to tell you about the routine, the lifestyle, the people and the places that make up real political life, at least here in the UK. I want you to see what it is really like so you can feel part of it, so you can see the glimpses of humour and pathos that build our political discourse and so you can feel that the Palace of Westminster is not a fiction like Hogwarts and that members of Parliament are neither all evil like Voldemort nor perfect like Hermione Granger. Because it has never been more important – in my lifetime at least (and bear in mind I grew up under Thatcher) – that the people genuinely take back control of politics.

I dedicated this book to my brother Luke because while I was writing it, Luke got a first-class honours degree from Birmingham University in political science. He started his degree while still using heroin, crack and cocaine. He had been addicted to drugs for at least twenty-five years. 'I'm going to university' sounded like another pipe dream in his chaotic life that I thought would inevitably disappoint. He is now three years clean and sober. He said to me once, 'I study politics. That's different to what you do; I actually know what I am talking about.' He mainly wanted to take the piss out of me but he makes a good point: the study of politics and the realpolitik are different. One is about theory and the other is about people's actual lives.

My brother Luke needed politics to give a shit about him and politics needs people like my brother to give a shit about politics, otherwise ordinary people with complex lives will always be failed. Politics is for everyone, so thank you for picking up this book and deciding to take part. Let's pull back the curtain and see what is really going on.

I

People Care About Potholes: Getting Elected

Elections are the very best part of political life and the very worst. They highlight the camaraderie and friendship within politics at the same time as bringing out all the demons of political battles. They are full of misleading spin, downright lies, tittle-tattle and grand promises, while simultaneously being the best example of a politician properly back among their people and responding to their needs.

I have stood in three general elections in six years in Parliament. I should only have stood in two. In the UK, government is required by law to call an election at least every five years. However, the Conservative government of the past decade has been quite trigger-happy with elections, which has led to three different prime ministers in the space of five years. Elections often cause political turmoil and uncertainty but I guess they are the only answer when politicians fail to act decisively and in the national interest. The only thing to do in that situation is to give that responsibility back to the people. Every single time a new general election was called, I was filled with a mixture of dread and delight. This was because I thought I would lose my job but I also absolutely bloody love an election campaign.

There is always the fear that the election will not go your way and you will find yourself out of a job. Politics is a risky business. In fact, I fear that one of the reasons we end up with the wrong people representing us politically is because the high stakes and the risk of possible public humiliation attracts the kind of people to public life who get a kick out of this. I don't think that risk-taking is always a bad thing – in fact, I attribute almost all my successes in life to my willingness to take a risk. Having my first son with a man I had only been going out with for a matter of weeks was, you could say, something of a risk. Deciding to essentially indebt my family to the tune of thousands of pounds in order to stand in an election was definitely a risk. My willingness to simply say, 'Sod it, let's give it a go, what's the worst that can happen?' has undoubtedly opened up opportunities that many sensible people would have overthought and avoided. I am not anti-risk.

However – and it is a big however – since becoming a member of Parliament, I have seen some of the stupidest risks taken by politicians because they obviously just liked the thrill of a possible public shaming. In my view, anyone who thinks that it is a good idea to send a picture of their genitals to an unknown person they have been chatting to on the internet must know they are going to get caught. Ministers are always being caught out in a 'text and tell' story where they have committed to writing something that they should not have been up to in the first place. Every single time this happens, someone will ask me, 'Gosh, how did they think that they were going to get away with it?' And I always give the same answer: they knew they were going to get caught and that was part of the thrill.

The first rule of politics is basic: learn to count (in other words, if you cannot win a vote, don't push it). The second rule of politics speaks to the more secretive nature of the plotting that goes on: never write anything down. My WhatsApp status is 'ready for the leaks'. If you wrote it, if you did it, you are going to have to own it – and someone always tells!

I cannot help but think that the political process lends itself to people who are drawn to risk, and I would say that is a near universal type in MPs. The way that this manifests, however, is different depending on the individual: some thrive on the adrenaline of being brave and bold and speaking truth to power; for others the attraction to risk and humiliation means that they use their platform to act sleazy. It is no surprise that politicians often get caught with their pants down; it is the risk of exposure that no doubt thrills.

The fact that Westminster attracts those who like to take risks affects our politics way beyond the sex-pest texting scandals. If the risk is mixed with entitlement and privilege (which in politics it so often is) then we have a dangerous combination, and we start to see politicians taking risks not just with their own personal or political lives, but with the lives of those across the country. Election campaigns are an absolute breeding ground in which the risky operator can make big brash statements.

Electioneering in this country and many others is all about taking risks, making big statements and pumping out messaging, therefore the people who are good at it are usually those who can take the biggest risks, make the biggest statements, puff out their chests the most. Electioneering is often reduced to politicians wearing hard hats and talking about building something or standing in front of a building that they claim they built, even if they had naff all to do with it. It makes for a good picture, but does very little in terms of engineering change.

A fundamental problem in our democracies is that many of these risk-taking, sloganeering individuals who are attracted to running for election have never had to face the consequences of a risk gone bad. Their houses have never been repossessed, they have never found themselves with not enough money to put petrol in the car or heard the 'thunk' of the electricity switching off. Over the time I have been involved on the front line of politics, the people who have risen to power and prominence have been those who don't understand that gambling has a stake and you can lose it because they will never feel the pain of the loss.

The trouble is, of course, that this is compounded when so many of our MPs come from backgrounds of privilege, because no matter what happens to our economy, no matter what happens to our public services, no matter what happens at our borders, they will never feel the downside in their daily lives. They don't need a good state school place for their kids. They are removed from that reality. So the risk to the public becomes quite significant, while the risk to the politicians themselves is just winning or losing in the game of politics.

The financial cost alone of getting elected is huge, especially if you put yourself forward in a marginal seat as I did, and very few people realise the reality of that. People often think that a) candidates are paid by their political parties – they are not; b) all people who stand for elected office are rich – many are (see above), lots are not; c) political parties give you loads of money to run your campaigns in your constituency – I bloody wish.

For me to be elected to Parliament cost my family around £40,000. Not in money we had in the bank you understand – we have never and will never have £40,000 in a bank account. And even if we had, I would have found it difficult to ask my husband to invest it in an election campaign that had a 50/50 chance of success. The cost for us was in our loss of earnings.

In 2013, two years before the 2015 election, I was selected to be the candidate for the Labour Party in Birmingham Yardley, a seat held at the time by the Liberal Democrats. In that time, I had to work without an office or base to raise the money, build an army of volunteers and get myself known by a population of 120-odd thousand people, all while holding down a job at a local women's charity, being a city councillor and bringing up my five-year-old and eight-year-old sons with my husband, who worked nights as a lift engineer.

The first thing that had to go was my full-time job, so I started to work part-time in order to have at least one day per week to focus on campaigning. By the end of the campaign, I had reduced my hours even further and for the final three months I was on unpaid leave and using any holiday days I had left. This cost me around £15,000 in the time I was campaigning. The real kicker for my family, though, was my husband's wage loss. As a lift engineer, he earned a premium for working a twelve-hour night shift. After I was selected, it became very clear that there was no way this could continue.

Tom's shifts were different each week and he worked two out of every four weekends, but most of my campaigning was done in the evenings after I had finished work and at the weekends and someone had to be at home to look after our kids. Unlike so many other politicians, we could not afford a live-in nanny and evening state childcare isn't a thing. Of course, my dad and my in-laws helped when they could but they were still working themselves so to ask them to stay every night of a week until 11 p.m. was too much. So my decision to stand for office meant that my lovely, dependable, breadwinning husband had to quit the night shifts and work a normal 9–5 job, costing his income £10,000 per year of the campaign. The rest of the cost is the money you end up investing in the campaign yourself. I bought many a leaflet on my personal credit card. And unfortunately, alongside all this, the bank doesn't accept requests to cut your mortgage to the same extent that your wages have been cut.

So, between us, we were £35,000 down, in mounting debt and all the while knowing that I might not win the seat. We sacrificed a lot to get me to Westminster and it could all have been for nothing.

I am pretty sure there has got to be a better election system than one such as this, that financially impoverishes a young family if they wish to get involved. It is not just a matter of the hardship this system brings to prospective candidates but the fact that it ensures that politics is a game that is only played by the very rich – or, as in my case, by potentially foolish idealists.

I don't want people to think I received no resource from my political party; I did. However, over the two-year campaign period it amounted to around £10,000 for materials and technology. If you are lucky and have a target seat, they may also fund a part-time campaign manager for you to share with someone else. You also usually get an injection of cash during what we call 'the short campaign' (the six-week period prior to the election) so you can post out loads of lovely glossy materials featuring your tiny face and the leader of your party's massive face. However, the candidate is expected to fundraise the lion's share of the campaign finances as well as run the campaign, work on the campaign, write the leaflets and, in my case, spend literally all night printing all the leaflets in an office so small and so hot that on one occasion, 3 a.m. saw me slaving over the fast photocopier in only my bra and pants.

A huge part of what you have to do during an election campaign is inspire people to come along and help. The emotional labour of trying to be hopeful and inspiring in front of rooms of student activists or local people can be pretty draining when you are running on four hours' sleep a night, your boss's patience is wearing thin with all the phone calls you are getting at work, you've had to bin 40,000 leaflets because they printed with the wrong year for the election and your kids are moaning about having to spend all weekend at the Labour Party, which is nothing like an actual party as there is neither a cake nor a magician in sight. It's hard to remain energetic and cheerful but if you don't drum up that support then on election day you'll be trying to knock 25,000 doors in a day with just the old party stalwart (who can only knock on three doors an hour because they get into a row about the Trident nuclear deterrent at every door) and another campaigner from the area who is still pissed off that they are not the candidate and deep down are waiting with bated breath for you to fail. So, you slick on some red lippy, turn your phone to silent and spend half your evenings standing in front of a crowd of people telling them that another future is possible.

And yet, amazingly, when you look back on all those years as a candidate, before you ever entered the hallowed halls of Westminster, you will only really remember the good times. Of course, this is not the case for those who don't get elected – many of those whom I stood alongside in the 2015 election who were unsuccessful naturally feel very differently. But for me, the hazy spell of nostalgia means I mostly remember the moments when something went well. For every leaflet that contains an embarrassing mistake,* there is the message that hits home and gets optimistically repeated back to you by the people that you meet. For every angry person who tells you that you are scum (or, in my favourite ever case, a voter who told me he would never vote Labour because he hadn't liked the way Labour Prime Minister Ramsay MacDonald had governed the country some fifty years before I was born), there is someone on a doorstep who says, 'I've never voted Labour before but I knew your nan and you are one of us so I am going to give you a shot.' The memories that stay with you from an election campaign are the late nights laughing with your volunteers after another hilarious day on the doorstep or the killer putdown you

---

* In the 2019 general election, Claudia Webbe, standing in a Leicester constituency, very commendably called on the government to invest in local education. Unfortunately, her leaflet actually called for 'incest in Leicester schools'. That is one hell of a typo.

managed to land against your opponent in the debates and hustings. A bit like childbirth, when you win an election or hold your baby in your arms, the fact that you can no longer feel your feet, you have given up on sleeping and you find most of those around you obscenely annoying all slips away.

An election campaign is a game of two halves. There are two very distinct periods that I would call the long-term campaign and the short campaign once an election has been called. The long-term campaign has no distinguishable start point. If you are a good political activist, you will be campaigning in your seat from the day after you won the last election, or lost it, or from the day you decide you might one day want to be the candidate. This essentially looks like door knocking every weekend, holding a couple of public meetings a month and trying to put out a letter or leaflet in your area every couple of months.

We rely on volunteers to deliver these pieces of paper — which 90 per cent of people throw straight in the bin. I shall pause for a moment as I can hear those of you who have not used a plastic straw since 2018 balking at the idea that so much political literature is posted but only has, if you are lucky, a 10 per cent readership. Believe you me, I am also annoyed about this for all sorts of reasons. But if you do not communicate with your constituents telling them what you are doing in their area with an element of regularity, they will express their annoyance with you, whether they would have read your leaflet or not. And these leaflets matter all year round because even if your residents don't read them, they make people feel that you are still there. Now, I am flattered that my constituents long for photos of me squatting and looking sad about a pothole but I wish more than anything that this was not the case because of the resource intensity of their production and delivery. I cannot afford paid delivery and it is very hard to keep volunteers motivated when you ask them to walk many miles every week delivering leaflets about bins. I wish that having a cracking Facebook page, a whip-smart Twitter account and a good email list was enough to properly reach all the people in my constituency, but it isn't – yet. People like to see you with potholes.

I know this was never covered on *The West Wing*; I cannot tell you how many political dramas I have watched where I have shouted at the telly, 'Why do you never see anyone stuffing envelopes?' But the truth is, people like parochial politics and they want it on a leaflet. The first political party that offered drop kerbs for all or a comprehensive tree pruning service in every neighbourhood would win a general election in the UK by a landslide. If you think that people hated the European Union, you have never heard them talk about the state of their neighbour's garden.

Anyway, I digress. The long campaign is all the political things that you do to build up a brand in readiness for the next election. It sounds cynical to write it down in black and white. It makes it seem as if all the work to save a local hospital, for example, or to collect food donations for local families, is just so you can win an election. And in a way it is. Brand building will always sound brutal and capitalist but if your brand is 'cares about the community' then that is probably because you care about the community, and you want to win the election so you can do more of it.

Take the example of the maverick congresswoman in the US, Alexandria Ocasio-Cortez: she has a very strong brand of being one of the people, of caring about her neighbourhood and being tough in the battle to represent it. She wants to be seen as a woman who gives power back to the people. There is absolutely no doubt that she has whole teams working on that brand: social media strategists, data analysts, speech writers and the rest. Everything she wears and everything she does will push that brand. This doesn't mean it is fake or put on just to win votes. The brand a politician pushes in almost everything they do is usually fomented by their own political and life experience and is built around the reason they entered politics. Her brand is strong because it is true.

Others may manufacture a brand that will fit with their political party. A Conservative politician in the UK, for example, is never going to try to push a brand in their local community built around fighting for the rights of immigrants or ensuring that more social housing is built to end the homelessness problem, even if they think this would be the right course of action, because if they were elected they would immediately come unstuck when they were forced to vote against this brand. Instead, they will work to build a brand that is about business and affluence in the local community, in line with their party politics. They probably don't want to be seen as maverick but rather as competent, dependable – dare I say it, even a bit boring. Boring works in lots of places. Remember, people care about potholes.

The long campaign for me involves lots of local campaigning where I try to find out what issues matter to my residents and address them. This is stuff like working with a local young woman sexually assaulted in an underpass to build up a local campaign to get rid of the underpass and fighting for more resources to keep our streets safe. I make every political act that I take on about the people I represent, always linking back the national picture to real stories of the people that I live among.

I am lucky to have a big national profile – in fact, scrap that, I am not lucky; I worked really hard in order to build a bigger platform and that has had huge benefits for the people I represent. It has also helped me in my long campaign because the leaflets matter less if people see you on their telly at night or when they open their papers. They feel, rightly, that you are out there fighting for them. At election time, I don't have to work very hard for people to know I am local or that I am tough and will battle on their behalf – they have seen it for years on their TV screens and in the stuff they read.

Obviously, having a big platform also carries a certain risk. Being so prominent gives your opponents an easy line of attack, especially if you are a woman. In the 2017 general election, my main opponent, the Liberal Democrat who had held the seat before me, tried to go hard on the fact that I was on the telly a lot, implying that I cared more about publicity than I did about my constituency. The attack was essentially designed to make me look like a show-off, more interested in frippery and fame than serving my community, but the truth is that having an MP who is a bit famous is not a bad thing for my constituents. It gives me a bigger platform, a voice that is harder to ignore, a call that can quickly rally an army to a cause. Anyone who tells you that as a representative you should seek to be less well known is either foolish or jealous.

This particular Lib Dem attack only told half the story. For example, one leaflet put out during the election took issue with the fact that I had been giving a book talk on the Saturday before the election. Had one of my constituents not been able to access help and support on that Saturday morning, this would of course have been a problem. However, despite what politicians might want you to believe, we don't do everything on our own; we have teams of caseworkers and campaigners standing alongside us, so if I am at a book event, a hospital appointment or just having a bloody rest, there is usually a system in place to make sure my constituents receive the same service as normal.

All the campaigning that happens in the run-up to the election essentially boils down to two things. First, building a brand and message that will cut through for both you as an individual representative and your political party as a national force. And second, finding out where your voters are so you can get them out to the polls on election day. The public are way more familiar with the process of the former than they are with the latter. As a local politician, you have a lot of control over the individual brand you build up locally, as a decent human and representative, but almost infinitesimal control over what happens with your political party nationally.

In the 2017 and 2019 general elections, I wish I had a pound for every time someone said to me, 'I like you, Jess, you helped my family when we needed you, but I just cannot vote Labour because I don't want Jeremy Corbyn to be prime minister.' This is crushing for a local politician – whether you agree with your party direction or not. So much of your time is spent trying to assert the local instead of the national but the truth is, no matter how big my ego, no matter how much I think the work I do locally matters, personal brand will amount for pretty much 10 per cent of my vote, maximum. This matters in the margins if you have a closely contested seat, so I don't want to undermine it, and I certainly spend the vast majority of my political life leaning in to it, but you as an individual are largely in the lap of your political gods.

Message discipline in a general election matters much more than you would think, and that is why political parties spend millions coming up with very annoying three- to five-word slogans to push out constantly. Personally, I hate this, and when watching election coverage, I balk every time someone says the slogan. But it works. Locally you can try to skewer it, so in the local hustings I have in the past asked the audience to shout out a number every time my opponent says 'long-term economic plan' or 'take back control'. This level of mischievousness only works on a small scale, though, and the truth is that this style of political messaging is effective and we all do it.

Pushing a single message works. In the 2015 general election, when I was fighting to win my seat for the first time, on every single piece of paper I sent through my constituents' doors or in any interaction I had with them I would remind them that my opponent had voted for the Bedroom Tax (thousands of my constituents suffered) on the same day he voted for tax cuts for wealthy people like him. By election day, people were repeating this fact to me as if it would be the first time I had ever heard it: 'You'll never guess what, Jess, that Lib Dem voted for the Bedroom Tax on the same day he voted for a tax cut for the wealthy.' Political messaging and branding works.

2

Get Out the Vote: Why Your Vote Counts

Then the big day arrives. The UK uses a voting system called 'first past the post'. The party who wins the majority of the 650 seats held by individual MPs wins the election overall. As a political activist, much of the work that you do leading up to an election is to give you an idea of where your voters are and how you can activate them to vote on election day. I must make it clear here that all the work you do as an MP is separate from your political campaigning and the contact details of anyone who comes to you with a problem or a policy issue cannot and must not be used in any way on election day.*

Obviously, in reality, there is some crossover – if you have helped a family out of homelessness in your role as an MP, then the likelihood is that they will think favourably

---

* In an election period I am not an MP. When an election is called and Parliament is dissolved, the position of MP ceases to exist. On election day, I have the exact same status as any other person who appears on the ballot, even if they are a man dressed up as a fish finger. I am not allowed to use the word MP on any literature; I have to cover up the sign on my office that says MP and I have to pay the rent on it which would normally be covered by Parliament as an expense. In an election I am just Jess, parliamentary candidate.

of you when it comes to the ballot, but you cannot use that information to contact them on election day. For a start, this would give a massive and unfair advantage to the sitting MP, but also, if this were the case, you can bet your bottom dollar that some would only help those who voted for them. A big part of my constituency work is done for people who will never vote for me – some out of choice but also because a huge number of people who live in my constituency cannot vote in the UK because they do not have British or Commonwealth citizenship or they are refugees. It would be a pretty shoddy MP who wouldn't help someone who was working in the country completely legally or who had fled a war just because that person can't vote for them.

As a political activist, however, in the weeks, months and years before an election you are building up a picture of where your voters are so that on election day you can knock their door, call their phone, drop them an email and get them out to vote. On any given election day in a local constituency, you and your team will make thousands of contacts. It can be quite an aggressive strategy to ring people in the morning to ask them if they have voted, then call them back at lunchtime and ask if they have done it yet and at dinner time check in again – until you have annoyed your constituents so much that they give in and go vote.

Using the phones is the quickest and most efficient way to do this but obviously you must have someone's phone number for that, so there is no replacement for knocking on doors. In all the elections I have stood in, there was just one when it did not rain pretty much all day. This means that volunteers turn back up at the campaign centres looking very dishevelled and sad. In the first election I ever stood in, I was wet through to my knickers by mid-morning and had to go home and change my clothes three times. I now always bring spare clothes. Lesson learned. It is vitally important that you put someone in charge of tea making and catering in every campaign centre (we always have at least three in the constituency). You will not keep volunteers knocking doors all day without sustenance, good humour and kindness; in Birmingham we call this socialism and samosas.

One of the main jobs you must organise on election day is giving lifts to people who cannot get to the polls themselves. This has dwindled in recent years with the increase in postal votes, but you still find yourself shouting from your phone station, 'Can someone go and fetch Mrs Jones on Clay Lane? She's hurt her ankle and her son can't come out to her today.' I kid you not, I have helped a woman get to the polling station who was in early labour. On election day, even if you have a majority of 10,000 votes and you are sure you will win, every single vote seems like it will be the one that makes the difference.

During the 2019 election, Anna, one of my team, tried to jazz up the car calls for the social media age by mimicking the famous James Corden *Late Show* Car Pool Karaoke where he films himself and celebrities singing along to hits. She wanted to film people being taken to the polls singing in a sort of celebration of democracy and turn it into a hashtag #CarPollKaraoke. However, the demographic of those who request a lift is such that she struggled to get Enid, 84, to agree to the stunt and Mabel, 91, didn't know the words to

Taylor Swift's 'Shake It Off'. I fear this seemingly good idea will forever remain on the cutting room floor of the Yardley Campaign Centre. One day, Anna, one day.

Before he lost his sight to macular degeneration, I used to make my dad be the chief driver on election day; he grew up in my constituency and so can chat happily with older residents about the streets they are driving down. Though he does not know the back catalogue of Taylor Swift, which is frankly his loss. On one occasion, he had been out of the campaign centre for an hour or so when a car call should just take twenty minutes, tops. When he finally returned, he explained that he had taken an older woman to vote as requested but on their return, she had asked him to change a few lightbulbs, which he did, and she then said she needed to get to the hospital for an appointment, so he had taken her and then waited to bring her home. That lady really made sure we worked for her vote.

As the candidate, you have an element of stardust about you, so my glitter is saved for all the people who are not sure for whom they are going to vote. On election day – and in fact for the weeks leading up to the election – I reserve my time to meet and speak to all the people who have said that they haven't made up their mind. Here is a tip: if you want a lot of attention from your local politicians, keep them guessing; similarly, if you want to be left alone, just say you are certainly voting for the other guy, whether or not you are. Some people are firmly ensconced in their political camp but lots of people play the field. These people fascinate me and speaking to them always teaches me something about our country. Elections can be about data, numbers, margins and error but for me it is also the very best opportunity to really hear why people have doubts, hopes and fears.

The only problem with this is that psychologically it can be a challenge when the conversations you decide to prioritise are all uncertain ones and, as a result, I get a very warped sense of how well the campaign is going. This is part of a phenomenon we in the business call 'candidates' disease'. It essentially means that you might have thousands of pages of data that tell you that you are definitely going to win; your opponent could have been caught with his (I say 'his' because my opponent has always been a man) fingers in the till or pictured in a sex dungeon hanging from a wall in suspender belts with an orange in his mouth and you will still think that you are definitely going to lose. It's like how a police car behind you in traffic will instantly make you feel guilty even though you're driving completely legally and safely. I guess it is the mind's way of preparing for the worst-case scenario. If you have contemplated the worst and walked through it in your mind it somehow makes it easier to cope with the dreaded uncertainty. Also, it means you get to act like a massive drama queen all day.

I guarantee you that the majority of candidates on election day will be preparing their concession speech in their heads and flouncing about in a melodramatic way, declaring, 'It's all over!' They may attempt to put a brave face on it, to keep the troops going out in the pouring rain to beg people to vote but inside they are assuming that, overnight, every one of the 70,000 people who live in their area has been in a massive WhatsApp conversation about what a loser they are.

So, at the end of every day during a campaign, we tally

up all the people we have spoken to and count how many are voting for me so I don't think everyone is having a collective wobble. On election day in 2015, having spent all day speaking to undecideds, I was convinced that I had lost. Caroline, who runs my campaigns like a data wizard, sat me down like a child and said very slowly and calmly to me, 'Today we have spoken to over 15,000 people who said they would vote Labour and then did and twelve people said that they voted against. You are acting like a crazy person.' Perspective is not high on my skillset when it comes to elections.

On election day, I campaign all day along with my activists. I stay until the bitter end with those volunteers committed enough not to feel awkward knocking on voters' doors until 9.45 in the evening. When the polls close at 10 p.m., the twenty or so of us still left in the office make our salutations of good luck before heading off to watch it all on the television like the geeks that we are. At that point, I head home and spend some time with my family and friends, listening to the exit poll on the radio as I drive home.

The exit poll is a survey that is done throughout election day by some very clever election experts and statisticians from Glasgow and Oxford Universities and is so called because they ask people exiting polling stations how they voted. The results of this are released at exactly 10 p.m. on the night of the election and they are declared quite dramatically over the bong of Big Ben that rings in the ten o'clock news on the television and the radio: 'Boris Johnson will have a majority of over seventy.' It is one of the most evocative soundbites from history to hear the exit poll result over the tolling of the bell. The sound of Big Ben is something I am very familiar with, given where I work, but on election night it can sound like a death knell or a peal of hope. In every national election that I have stood in, the exit poll has been almost exactly right, much as I wish this hadn't been the case.

And finally we have the sampling and the count. The count is that bit on the telly on election night that is held in the local sports hall or exhibition space, where hundreds of people are lined up on long tables counting all the votes that have been cast. I bloody love an election count, especially the ones where I am not a candidate.

First and foremost, I would like to disavow you of the very first myth of an election night. In 99 per cent of cases (all but those where the result is very close – within a thousand votes in a general election and a hundred in a small local election), all of the professional candidates (discounting the guy dressed up as a fish finger or a bloke with a bucket for a head) from political parties know the overall result before the votes are actually counted.

I love that up and down the country people stay up late to watch the results coming in and political pundits live from the studio in London interrupting their guessing game chit chat with the words, 'I am sorry, Ken, I'll have to interrupt you – we must go live to Bury St Edmunds where the results are about to be declared.' The truth is that the moment on the telly where the local mayor reads out the results is not the first that the candidates have heard of it. Not by a long chalk. In every election I have ever stood in, I have known whether I have won for at least three hours by that point. In this, and so many other regards, politics is nothing like *Britain's Got Talent*.*

Before the votes are counted, they are all tipped out on to the table, unfolded and sorted so that they are all facing the same way up, and stacked in groups of twenty-five ballots so they can be counted more easily. This gives a pretty good indicator of who's won. If you really want to annoy the people counting the votes, you could fold up your ballot into a tiny square, or even turn it into an origami crane if the mood takes you. I have seen thousands of ballots in my life and am yet to see any origami. Please do express yourself; it's moments like this that cheer up what is a very long night, after a very long day.†

Each polling area (linked with the polling station that you vote in) is sorted separately and kept separate, so that when they are counted, we know exactly how many votes come from each area. While all this unfolding, sorting and piling is going on, teams of political party activists stand in front of the table with clipboards, pens and special charts taking a sample of the votes as they see them. This is called sampling. The sampling will never be perfect, it will never be completely

---

* We once received a letter calling for my husband to attend the audition in Birmingham for *Britain's Got Talent* with his act Tom's Turkish Dance Extravaganza. To this day, I do not know which of his mates went to the bother of entering him. He is often mistaken for being Turkish, however he has no discernible Turkish dance talent.
† If you live in Newcastle or Sunderland in the UK, please make your ballot into an origami crane. These two places always compete to be the first to declare a result on election night and are proper try-hards. There is no constituency it would annoy more to have to unravel a load of beautiful Japanese-inspired paper craft.

accurate; however, a decent and experienced activist who has done this many times before can get a good read from a couple of hundred votes – enough to confidently say that in this particular polling area, 70 per cent voted Labour, 15 per cent voted Conservative and 15 per cent was split across other parties. (I wish they were all like this. Alas, they are not.)

Once an activist has a decent sample, they will run it up to another activist who is sat with a spreadsheet showing how each different area voted in the most recent election and it soon becomes pretty clear if you have won, lost or if it is too close to call. In reality, if you know the area you are counting for well – which you bloody well should – you don't even need the spreadsheet. In the 2017 election, when I ended up with a huge 17,000 majority, we knew I had won because in one of our toughest areas, where we never win, I had nearly 60 per cent of the vote on the sample.

The sampling process at an election count is the most exciting moment of the night. Bear in mind of course that the people who are doing the sampling are usually your best, most trusted activists and they will have been up since six in the morning and been out encouraging people to vote for at least twelve solid hours. They will almost certainly have been drenched in the rain, been on their feet more than off them, have only eaten packets of sandwiches and crisps (and in Birmingham, though I cannot speak for elsewhere, the obligatory samosas). And then, around midnight and into the early hours of the next day, they get their heads down for around two hours to see if it has all been worth it. And all this is before the votes even start being officially counted. Election counts are incredibly secretive undertakings.

While there are television cameras, photographers and reporters at them, you are not allowed to film or take pictures or
talk about the individual ballots. This would break all kinds
of election laws. For this reason, no phones are allowed into
the main hall where votes are being counted. If you are seen
with a phone in your hand it takes about a minute before a
very officious council employee gives you a telling off. There
are always police officers at counts in the UK making sure
that should there be any breaches of democratic laws they are
on hand to deal with them – or fights, which, believe me,
happens more than you might think. My own father was once
thrown out of an election count with his mate after a bit of a
scuffle. Tensions are high at the count and the political parties
are all there emblazoned with the rosettes of their tribe.

Once the sampling is done, the event then turns into a long
night of sitting around. In my experience, Liberal Democrats
are the best prepared: they always seem to have camping
chairs, flasks and plentiful snacks. This means that the atmosphere at an election count can swing from one moment
feeling as if you are in a scene from *The West Wing*, at the
front line and cutting edge of an exciting shift in democracy,
to being at what looks like the tea tent at a rainy summer fete
with dishevelled septuagenarians passive-aggressively asking,
'Are you using that chair?'

It's only at this point that the votes are actually counted.
Except, that is, for the vast number of (sometimes creatively)
spoiled ballots, which are not counted until the end of the
process. One day I want to produce a fancy coffee table book
of the best spoilt ballots that I have ever seen. In America,
there is an option on a voting paper to 'write in' a candidate's

name but, alas, we do not have this option in the UK. If I had a pound for every time someone has said to me that there should be an option of 'none of the above' at the bottom of the ballot I could give up political life and buy a small cottage in the countryside. As this option is not available to them, many of the British public often express their frustration or flair through spoiling their ballot.

While I think everyone should take advantage of their right to vote and use it properly, I also think that if you really don't want to vote for any particular candidate, going along to the polling station and spoiling your ballot is a far more noble option than just opting out and not bothering to vote. It also plays a much more important role in our democracy than people realise. If you do not bother to turn up to the polling station, to have your name ticked off the list as a person who voted, it is very likely that you will fall out of the political system all together.

In the UK, people register to vote and the people who turn up are entered onto what we call 'the marked register', and after each election I get a huge data file of all the people who voted. So, as I approach your front door to speak to you (as politicians love to do), I know whether you vote or not. I know whether you vote in local elections or just national elections, or if you love a bit of referendum voting. For those people not on the marked register, however, the likelihood is that no political party will ever bother with them. There are 70,000 doors in my constituency and it is hard to get around them all. I would like to spend time talking to people who don't vote, to find out why they feel disenchanted with democracy, but time simply doesn't allow, and this makes our system poorer in my view because it pushes people who are disengaged further out from a system that will certainly affect their lives.

Therefore, I feel a fondness for a spoilt ballot because even though the people who spoil their ballots didn't want to pick any of the candidates for whatever reason, they did remain part of the political ecosystem. This is the noble reason that I like them but if I were to be truly honest, I also like them because they are a moment of light relief on election night.

I read every single one of the spoilt ballots cast in my constituency. This is not rare – in fact, most candidates do and someone representing every candidate has to. The returning officer (the person who manages the election count, usually a local council official) collects all of the spoilt ballots and each of the candidates or their representatives huddle around to inspect them. This process happens so you can all agree that the ballot is truly spoilt and argue the toss if you think that the person casting the vote has made a clear preference for one of the candidates. You essentially get to fight for the spoilt ballots to be included in your vote tally.

The obvious and uncontested spoilt ballots are usually that someone has left the whole piece of paper blank, or the 'none of the above' voter who just draws a double or single strike across the ballot showing they hate you all. Those are uncontested and unamusing.

The second category, and I am pleased to say it is common up and down the British Isles, is the 'cock and balls' category. As we are a nation that, when asked, voted for 'Boaty McBoatface' to be the name of a state polar exploration ship, it should not surprise too many people that in every election I have stood in there has been more than a smattering of ballots that are spoilt with the ancient symbol of the penis.

Now, the penis markings are more contestable. If a voter has drawn a penis next to the name of a candidate or in the box allocated for a vote preference, it could be legitimately argued by that candidate that there is a clear mark next to their name and therefore a voting preference. Members of the British public take note: *any mark in the box where you are meant to draw a cross can count as a vote for that candidate.* So, if you are drawing a penis next to the name of a person you think is a cock, you may very well be accidentally voting for them and they can argue the toss on that (pun totally intended). Equally, but less controversially, if someone ticks the box instead of marking with an 'X', while this is considered a spoilt ballot, you simply argue that the person (quite clearly) intended to vote for you and you always win this argument.

In most of the elections I have stood in there have been around 120 spoilt ballots (on one occasion, the spoilt ballots beat an independent candidate) and around twenty of them are usually reallocated to one of the candidates. I have never needed to fight particularly hard to be allocated the spoilt votes because by this point in the night, the margin I had won by was large enough for it not to matter. However, my dad told me a story about a local election in the 1980s where the margin was less than ten votes and he spent some time arguing that the ballot which had 'Fuck the Tories' scrawled across it was a clear indication of a vote for Labour. Reader, he did not win this battle. But if I were ever to be in an election with such a narrow margin and someone had drawn a penis next to my name, I promise you I would be arguing for that vote.

These are the most common spoilt ballots that you encounter on election night, along with a smattering of 'you're all crooks', 'what's the point in voting' and other such grumblings. Some people go to extraordinary lengths and write a whole essay across their ballot – and I want to reiterate that I read every single one because I think that they are important and, no matter how ridiculous some of them are, they speak to the feelings in our country about the electoral system.

On one occasion, I saw a ballot in a local police and crime commissioner election where the voter had been so opposed to the idea of police and crime commissioners (can't say I blame them) that they had gone to the bother of designing and ordering a specific rubber stamp that read 'police and crime commissioners are a waste of money' and gone along to a voting booth with said stamp and an ink pad and stamped every inch of their ballot paper with their message. That level of commitment shows a strength of feeling that is hard to ignore. Mind you, in the same election, someone had also decided that they wanted the US-style option of writing in their own candidate to vote for and had written in at the bottom 'Kate Middleton's Haunted Vagina' and then voted for her. To be honest, it was a welcome relief to see the female anatomy getting a look-in on the spoilt ballot front.

I am conscious of the fact that I have described a huge and beautiful democratic process as if it is a clinical recipe: message, volunteers, debate, knock doors, rosette, ballots, repeat.

But the most important person in an election is you and that is why they are beautiful and brilliant. In an election I get one vote, just like you do.* For one day, we are all equals, with an equal stake in our country. In the weeks that lead up to that one day, what you say on the doorstep, in a survey response, in an email or online, really matters to those of us branded with party political motifs. We pore over every word, every nuance, we feed it back and we try to improve. I have frequently texted the leader of my political party with the information I am hearing on the doorsteps.

During an election, your voices ring out and it can be deafening, but that is why a system with all sorts of fault lines and failures is good. An election is a reset button. We hear the loud angry mob and the quiet reserved suggestion. It is like a political Glastonbury festival for a few weeks, where the most important thing for each of us is our collective future, and I love it. The highs and lows are all driven by the demands for us to be better and do better and you, each and every one of you, are the most important person. The power shifts back from a dusty palace in London to your living room and for as long as I take part in this process, nothing – no fancy parade of the Queen in her crown past my office, or brilliant speech on the steps of Westminster Hall by a US president, or glitzy award ceremony – will ever be as thrilling as you saying to

* This is not strictly true in that I usually have at least one or two proxy votes, so I vote on behalf of someone who is ill or has been called away for work. We find these people while we are door knocking and canvassing for votes, or some people call my office and request that we arrange a proxy for them as they trust us to vote how they want. As yet, I have only been asked by people who want to vote for me but honestly, hand on heart, if one of my constituents asked me to vote for the other guy on their behalf, I would do it. If you believe in democracy that must mean something.

me on election day, 'Don't worry, bab, I voted on the way to work this morning, so I have done my bit.' It is everything I believe in; every late night and time away from my kids, every bad headline disappears on election day because it is about us doing something together.

I have stood on hundreds of doorsteps over the years with people who have told me that they just can't be bothered to vote, that they don't see the point or don't feel they know enough about it. I would rather people shouted in my face and told me that they will not be voting for me and will be voting for my opponent because they hate me than hear that people will not vote. Every campaigner worth their salt will have pulled out one of the following arguments to try to persuade the disenchanted citizen:

- Women died so that all women like you would have the power to have an equal say in how our country is run. (I have literally stood on a doorstep acting out in charade style the death of suffragette Emily Wilding Davison at the Epsom Derby. I fear it had limited success.)
- Right now across the world, people are risking their lives in order to vote in their countries. People are fleeing their homes, lives and businesses because oppressive regimes won't allow them to vote. All I am asking is that you walk three minutes to the local school on the way to work; these people have walked across continents for such freedom. Yes, I know it's raining; here, borrow my umbrella.
- If you don't vote you can't complain when things

happen that you don't like. (This is probably untrue and they know it.)

Obviously, I believe that the choice to take part or not is a vital plank in any good democracy but I still don't like it. When in schools talking to young people about voting, I ask them why they think that the contemporary Conservative Party massively inflated tuition fees, cut housing benefit to those under twenty-one and decided that the minimum wage rate should start at age twenty-five not eighteen. Usually they answer something derogatory about them being old fashioned and not having enough young people in their ranks to care. They are right, but frankly the fault does not lie solely at the feet of the politicians in that those politicians never have and never will rely on the vote of young people because those aged eighteen to twenty-four don't vote at anywhere near the rate of older people. Polling research from Ipsos MORI suggests that turnout in the 2019 general election ranged from 47 per cent among 18–24-year-olds up to 74 per cent among over-65s. Well then, who do you think policy makers are going to prioritise? Yes, we should govern for the whole country regardless of who votes, but let's be realistic here. If 74 per cent of 18–24-year-olds voted, I guarantee you the minimum wage would be the same for an eighteen-year-old as it is for a 65-year-old. Don't do it for me; do it for you. If you don't vote because you think 'no one is fighting for me', well, the best place to start that fight is in your own home.

Elections are won and lost by those who turn out to take part. The people who rub their hands in glee when the disenfranchised utter the words, 'You're all the same, I am not going to bother,' are the same people who have always had all the power. Those who have opted out have not struck a blow against an estranged and distant political elite; they have been swept to the floor like a little plastic soldier on the war game map. Elections matter – not just to geeks like me, but to all of us. So don't let a bit of rain mean you have your wages cut or can't get a doctor's appointment. Don't let a fool who got caught in a text-and-tell convince you that politics is broken. It's on us to fix it, so let's get out there and do it. God, I love an election.

3

What Does an MP Do All Day?

After winning an election, you arrive at Westminster, fresh-faced and full of excitement to change the world, as a member of the House of Commons. It baffles me that, although a job like mine is under so much scrutiny, is covered in hundreds of hours of footage week in week out, is the main feature of most news broadcasts, newspapers and many light entertainment shows, there is really very little understanding of what we do all day.

I am, however, writing this in 2020 and so the week I will describe is not typical of how I am working now, because there is absolutely nothing normal about the way that politics is operating in the pandemic. A 2020 week for an MP is a dull jaunt through a list of Zoom meetings, some of which occur in Westminster while you sit in the room next door to another person in the exact same meeting as you. For me, politics is about being in among people, a busy office full of constituents, days out wrapped up warm knocking on doors and going into people's homes, hearing their woes. Politics for me is about emergency meetings with a load of people to talk about getting something done. Shouting, 'Barbara, you're on mute, press the button at the bottom left!' is not the same.

During the pandemic, the government, in all its wisdom, decided that allowing members of Parliament to vote remotely, while completely logistically possible, was just not cricket. Instead, they thought that politicians should travel from all over the country, bringing with us our germs and various strains of the coronavirus, so that for approximately twenty minutes per day we could vote in a huge conga line that was allegedly socially distanced, albeit in a room that has no windows or ventilation. Of course, as soon as the cameras were turned away, people were backslapping and standing right on top of each other. By the time we actually reached where we would cast our votes, I had had to treat two of the most powerful men in the country as if they were my young sons ignoring the rules – 'How many bloody times do I have to tell you? Honestly, am I talking to myself?!'

So, I will take us back to 2019 and through a normal week of an MP. I must caveat this before I start: this is my normal week. Some undoubtedly do more. I imagine government ministers have a considerable amount more on their plates what with running a government department and all, though of course they have the civil service to help them. Some MPs, of all political persuasions, do a lot less. Some are bone idle. Occasionally, an MP will stand up in the House of Commons with a question only for everyone on the green benches to turn to their neighbour and ask, 'Who are they? I don't think I have ever seen that bloke before in my life.' Hey, maybe they are really good constituency MPs – or maybe they are the director of many different companies and that is taking up a huge amount of their bandwidth. I have no idea how this sort of MP structures their work–life balance because they are like submarines gloriously cruising along underwater, popping up occasionally to ask a question about roadworks on the A61.

Parliament sits from a Monday to Thursday in Westminster. On a Monday morning, I wake up in Birmingham. I don't pretend to live in Birmingham, I don't just represent the city; I live here. So, I wake up in Birmingham at 6.30 a.m. and, just like most parents, spend the first part of my day endlessly shouting about shoes and PE kit or reading out spellings. Actually, scrap that, that was a lie. If my husband were writing this he would say: 'You've missed out the first hour of the day where you lie on your side annoying me in bed going through messages and emails on your phone, checking Twitter, reading the headlines and making yourself stressed out so by the time the kids emerge from their rooms at around 7.30 you are in a foul mood and everything we request assistance with is met with either complete silence while you stare at your phone or you deliver a set of auto responses, such as, "In a minute, I'm just doing something for work."'*

Unfortunately this is true. It isn't just politics that does this to a person – anyone who has a high-pressure job and sleeps with their phone under their pillow will likely have a similar experience. I don't think there has been a morning since I was elected that I have not awoken with a gasp of anxiety about what the day will bring. When you are a politician and you are under so much scrutiny, a mindless tweet sent before you go to sleep can cause one hell of a storm by the time you wake. Or, while you were sleeping, journalists who manage

---

* My son Danny has taken to calling me Jess, which I hate, because he says that when I am in a phone coma I cannot hear the word 'mom' but 'Jess' can reach me. This makes my heart break.

the morning bulletins may have been texting you asking if you can come on to the *Today* programme at 7 a.m. because in some part of the world there has been a heinous murder, breakout of war, a terrorist attack or one of your colleagues has been arrested. Every morning when I open my eyes, I have to brace myself for controversy, hatred or the need to immediately have an educated opinion about something I have just this second heard about. Meanwhile, my children still need to be got ready for school.

I remember one morning waking at 5 a.m. to a message from a colleague that read, 'Oh my god, have you seen the news?' followed by a link to a newspaper article. Maybe it is egotistical or more likely paranoid but the first thing you think when you see a message like that is, 'Shit, what have I done? What have the papers found out about?' I am always preparing for my entire career and my family's security to blow up in my face at any minute. On this occasion it was the news about the then MP for Leicester East Keith Vaz who had been rumbled for paying for and sleeping with prostituted men at what seemed like a very dingy drug party. I turned over to my husband in bed and gave him a precis of the situation. With a heavy heart, I said, 'We are always just one story away from losing everything.' To which he replied in annoyed tones, 'Have you been sleeping with male escorts at parties with lots of drugs?' I shook my head. 'Well, shut up, turn your phone off and go back to sleep, woman.'

It is hard to explain this level of anxiety to someone who does not experience it. My husband is a painfully calm pragmatist and he thinks that worrying about stuff that might never happen is an entirely pointless and indulgent endeavour. He thinks that the news can just bloody well wait until the kids have had their Weetabix and been walked down the road to school. Of course, in many ways he is right: it usually can all wait, there is no need to react immediately to everything, to have an instant opinion on every little thing. But it doesn't feel like that to me. This is the reality of 24-hour news, social media and global politics: it drags you from bed every morning panting with anxiety.

After I have got over the initial heart palpitations, had a cup of tea and packed my kids off to school, I start my official working day. By this time, my phone will have at least thirty unread messages from: my staff about issues of the day; my colleagues commenting on the *Today* programme; journalists asking me for a comment or if I can do something for them; and my dad asking what he should get my son for his birthday in four months' time.

I shall pause here to introduce you to my team. Very often, my staff's wages are mistaken for cash that is paid directly to me. I get it; lots of MPs did terrible things in the expenses scandal – some even went to prison for it and they were rotters, no doubt. However, since I was elected in 2015, some six years after the expenses scandal, I have never worked under a system where you could put in claims for your new Teasmade, duck house or Persian rug willy-nilly and expect the taxpayer to fund it. I do receive a number of what are called expenses and every year when these are published, hundreds of people get in touch with me and complain that I am pocketing in excess of £150,000 for my own personal use. I am not. That budget pays for the five people who work for me – or, more accurately, work for the good people of Birmingham Yardley, helping them with their issues.*

Three and a half of the people I employ manage casework that comes into my Birmingham office from my constituents. By way of example, in 2020 I received 14,200 emails of casework from my constituents raising issues that they wanted my help with. The phone rings constantly throughout the day. I also operate an open office where three days a week people can come in and speak to someone in person and it is always full, with five or six people waiting to be seen at any given time. Some of the cases are about broken paving slabs and take half an hour to handle; some are about homeless families that take months if not years to sort out. I used to open my office five days a week but the demand meant that my caseworkers simply never had the time to take any action on the cases.

One of these three members of staff works on local campaigns and communications, and helps with gathering information from my constituents who don't come in. He helps my constituents to reach me, rather than me them, although all good political discourse should be a conversation rather than a broadcast from either side. He leads on local campaigns when there is an issue like rising knife crime in an area of my constituency or cuts to local school budgets.

---

* MPs' staff are employed directly by MPs; they are not employed by Parliament and, what's more, neither am I. I am paid by Parliament but I have no employer, per se. I have to file a tax return even though I pay my taxes as I go just like any employee. An MP's office is essentially a small business. This is one of the many reasons there are a lot of dodgy HR issues that go on with MPs' staff – if the MP you work for is a bullying sex pest, there is no real way out of that for the member of staff that doesn't involve them losing their job.

He helps me to get people together to change stuff and raise the voices of my constituents.

In London I have one and a half members of staff. One leads on policy casework, which is separate to the kind of casework like, 'My mom lives in Yardley and has been a nurse in this country for twenty years and is about to be wrongfully deported to Jamaica, can you help?' and more like, 'I am writing as your constituent, to ask you to support the amendment on "parliamentary approval of trade agreements" in the Trade Bill when it returns to the Commons in the new year.' We receive thousands of pieces of policy casework every year and mostly this is driven by online petitions. Everyone receives a reply. In every case, I write to the relevant minister of state raising the issue my constituent cares about and then feed back to them on what was said. I often don't agree with my constituents and I am honest with them about this. I am regularly urged to vote one way or another on legislation of the week and I get letters demanding that I vote both for and against the same thing. My constituents, you may be surprised to hear, do not all agree with each other.

My policy caseworker also manages my diary, which has got to be the worst job in politics because I frequently go rogue and put in stuff myself. I wildly agree to almost anything I am asked to do and she then has to try to fit it all in. Regularly, I will send her messages like, 'Why am I speaking in rural Devon this weekend?', only for her to forward me the email I sent some weeks back, personally agreeing to speak at a meeting for no more than twenty people 200 miles from my home on a Friday night, like an idiot. I am a pain in the arse to diary manage.

In London, I also employ a woman who helps me to manage all the work that I do that has a national or international reach beyond my constituency. She works with me mainly on policy development and campaigning about violence against women and girls, youth violence, workplace harassment, children's safeguarding – and whatever else I have decided to wade my massive gob into this week. She also helps me build relationships with people affected by these things all over the country and the organisations and charities who represent them.

Because of my profile in fighting against domestic abuse, I receive thousands of emails every year from women all over the country sharing their frightening cases. I am afraid I hear the same story over and over again, with victims facing the same housing, welfare, courts and justice problems all over the country. There is a protocol in Parliament whereby MPs should not really take on cases from the constituency of another MP but, frankly, some MPs are useless and unhelpful, and I cannot bring myself to respond saying, 'Sorry, your MP thinks it is okay that you have been living in a Travelodge with three kids for nine months and it's not my problem because I'm not your MP.' Others don't necessarily want help but they want me to know about their situation so that it can inform my work on abuse and violence. I need a member of staff to help me manage all of these stakeholders and work with them so that not only can we try to help them where possible (sadly, often we can't) but also to keep a record and find stories that will help us fight for improvement.

All of the people who work for me do an incredibly emotionally draining job and they are not very well paid because

I am only given a limited budget to pay them. I receive the exact same budget as an MP whose constituency might have half the number of people living in it and not even 10 per cent of the poverty and social housing issues Yardley contends with. I have to employ more caseworkers who handle more cases and get paid less than a caseworker in a more affluent constituency. I do not have a communications person who handles the press for me; I do that. I do not have anyone to write speeches for me; I do that. I don't have a chief of staff or someone who can follow me around ensuring I am briefed for every meeting; I do that. My staff do an absolute shit tonne of work for my constituents. They are rarely praised or recognised by the public and people think that everything that gets done is down to me. It isn't even half me; I am one in our team of six people. They deserve better pay and better recognition for all that they do.

Having said all of that about how smashing they are, let's go back to the many messages they have sent me by 9 a.m. on a Monday that read, 'Just a quick one, when you have a minute, can you tell me definitely what you think about investment in carbon capture?' Or, 'Wondered what you thought about us opening this weekend and making hot meals for the people living in hotels – let me know your thoughts.' Messages like this persist throughout the day but on a Monday morning they are usually catching up after the weekend so there are more and I read them as I make my way to get on the train to travel to London.

I ignore people who call me when I am on the train because for some reason, I have decided that being on the train is a good excuse for ignorance. I won't beat myself up too much about this because even if I tried to take a call or use the internet on the West Coast Mainline, after three seconds I would be rudely reminded that although humankind put a man on the moon twenty-two years before I was born, we cannot make the Wi-Fi on a train actually work. Long may it peacefully continue.

I arrive at my office in Westminster at around 12.30. Parliament doesn't start until 2.30 p.m. on a Monday in order to allow members of Parliament to travel in from around the country. It may also be because historically many members of Parliament had second jobs. Of course, some still do and the late start allows them to do a bit of bricklaying in the morning – and by bricklaying, I mean of course being a non-executive director paid £100,000 for a few hours' work a week. No one is doing a spot of bricklaying on the side these days – well, not that they are declaring on the books. Perhaps Theresa May is excellent at repointing chimneys but she just does it for close friends and family.

Once I am in the office, I will usually catch up with my London-based staff for half an hour or so before the business of the day. Every day, Parliament opens with a question session. The most famous is obviously Prime Minister's Questions, which happens on Wednesday,* but every other day of parliament also opens with departmental questions on a rolling

---

* When I was a kid, PMQs was on a Thursday and I used to watch it with my nan while she did the ironing in our house, which she insisted on doing every Thursday even though no one asked her to – perhaps it was passive-aggressive side-eye at what scruffbags we all were. My nan never once wore a pair of trousers, was always impeccably turned out and cleaned her front step with bleach once a week. Never believe the lie that the working classes are the scruffy classes; in fact, as Boris Johnson proves time and again, the exact opposite is the truth.

rota, so Monday might be Home Affairs questions; Tuesday, the Treasury; Wednesday, Welsh questions (before PMQs); and Thursday, Women and Equalities questions. After that, we have ministerial statements and urgent questions, where Parliament wants answers from the government on the issues of the day. On Mondays, this means reacting to events that happened over the weekend, such as a large factory closure threatening thousands of jobs, rioting or the airing of a documentary that highlights the abuse of older people in care homes.

Fitted in and around all of this are the usually back-to-back meetings that go on until 7 p.m. Let's start with the committee meetings for All-Party Parliamentary Groups (APPGs). I am the chair of the domestic violence APPG, the co-chair of the women and work APPG and the sex equality APPG. I also sit on the child contact centres APPG, the modern slavery APPG, the sickle cell APPG and the homeless APPG. There is an APPG for everything.

There are also a seemingly infinite number of team meetings to attend. As the Labour spokesperson on domestic abuse and safeguarding, I attend the Home Affairs team meeting where we plan a strategy for what is coming up in the Commons and Lords, the media and elsewhere for the week. Then there are all the regional team meetings. We have a meeting of Birmingham Labour members and cross-party Birmingham team meetings. (During the pandemic, these took place at least twice a week and involved the head of the council and the chief executives and chairs of all the hospitals.) Then there are the West Midland region-wide representative meetings because, despite what

I might think, Birmingham is not the only place in the West Midlands.

Aside from the APPGs and the team meetings, there are also all the party meetings. Every Monday, we have the parliamentary Labour Party team meeting where all Labour MPs gather to be given direction by our shadow cabinet – or, for most of my years in Parliament, to give direction *to* our shadow cabinet and generally have a massive barney. Every other week, there is the women's parliamentary Labour Party, which I chaired for three years, where the women in the Labour Party work together to achieve change in both Parliament and the country and to ensure that women have a strong collective voice so we cannot be ignored.* Essentially, I am in many teams; it's a bit slutty, really.

I also have to factor in meetings with organisations and individuals who wish to lobby me about something from a national perspective rather than a local one. Every day, I will receive at least forty of these meeting requests – for example, from someone wishing to tell me about how arthritis policy needs changing or how more kids should be encouraged to play chess in school. If I were to meet with every one of these organisations, I would need an eight-day week where I never slept. There is simply no way that any MP could ever be active across everything that we are asked to care about. It must be narrowed down to things that you really care about or have a chance of changing. I spend a good eight hours a week talking to abuse charities and victims, for example. I will also make time for the meetings covering the issues that

* We are often still ignored.

many of my constituents care about, such as specific foreign affairs. Lots of my constituents care about issues in Kashmir, Palestine and the wider Middle East, for example, and many have concerns about specific sorts of cancer care.

Another way to sort the wheat from the chaff in the mountain of meeting requests is through the approach of those who ask to meet with you. If someone sends a really long round-robin email to all MPs and just changes our name at the top, they can expect to be waiting a long time for a meeting. If you want a voice in Parliament aside from your own local MP, then I recommend targeting your efforts towards those who have a record of speaking about your issue. Also, top tip, be really nice and engaging with the people who answer the phone and emails; they are the gatekeepers to our time. My staff will drop me a message saying something like, 'Lovely bloke called John just called and he wondered if you could pop into a meeting later about access to services for blind people. He was really polite.' My staff are on my team but you can make them be on yours too. Some callers are demanding, difficult and entitled; my staff will likely ignore them and their request, and who can blame them?

These meetings all take place in Portcullis House where members of the public can queue up and go through security in order to come and meet with us. Portcullis House is the ugly, modern part of Parliament. Although don't let the word 'modern' mislead you; it is not so modern that the heating is proficient or that panes of the glass from the glazed ceiling don't sometimes randomly tumble to the ground. The newer government buildings are falling apart just like the historic ones. Inside it looks like a large school hall with eateries around the edge and a hundred odd tables scattered across the floor. When it is alive with many meetings, as it is most days, the noise is reminiscent of a large municipal swimming pool. In the winter, meetings take on an air of mystery because when the building was designed with a glazed roof to let in the light, the fact that for at least four months of the year in the UK it is dark by 4 p.m. was overlooked. Recently, the building's management has taken to stringing up the kind of bright yellow lead lamps that you might see on a building site so that you have an outside chance of seeing the briefing paper that the National Association of Teachers has just handed over to you.

As you glide from meeting to meeting, between your office and Portcullis House, you will inevitably fill the brief windows of time chatting with other MPs hanging around the area and also the lobby journalists based in Parliament who are often scattered among the tables awaiting a passerby to have a good old gossip with. Many times I have seen a story written up in respectable national newspapers based on an idle chat I have had with a journalist while waiting in the coffee queue without even a thought that what I was saying might be noteworthy. If you read any political story and there is a quote from an unnamed MP, this has likely come from a chance encounter in Portcullis House.

The constant presence of lots of journalists in Portcullis House means that the more secretive plotting types of meetings usually take place in a Member of Parliament's office. And there is a lot of plotting that goes on in politics, lots of quiet little meetings without notetakers. This is usually where party politicking goes on and trying to find allegiances with others to make demands – sometimes of the government but, let's face it, a lot of this is to find a way to pressure your own political party to do what you want. Every single faction of politics does this plotting.* Think of a politician that you really admire, one who you really think the sun shines out of their bum – well, they're having off-the-record chats with colleagues to try to neuter another politician or powerful grouping. I am not very good at it because I am not very discreet or subtle, nor am I that arsed if someone knows my opinion of them, but I do it just like everyone does. You would be surprised how time-consuming it can be.

The other category of meeting that I will be attending on my Monday in Parliament is likely to be one with government ministers in which I am demanding that they explain themselves or lobbying them to change things. This happens much more than you would think. The sad reality of the politics that we see on our telly is that it simply doesn't show the amount of collaboration between MPs in different parties that goes on in order to achieve things. I would say that on average I have had a meeting with a minister pretty much every single week since I was elected. Sometimes these are incidental chats in the corridor about a specific issue, sometimes they are meetings arranged well in advance by ministers' private offices.

The small section of Parliament that most people see is the adversarial shouting match shown on the television where MPs shred each other's ideas or seek to have a 'gotcha'

---

* This very text will inevitably be sent to me as an image on Twitter in the future by someone wanting to prove what a snake in the grass I am and how I was plotting the overthrow of Jeremy Corbyn all along.

moment by tripping up a minister. In my experience, this has rarely been successful in changing anything. Progress usually happens through lots and lots of meetings where you sit with ministers, civil servants and experts and gently encourage them to do the thing or undo the thing you want.

I remember once a group of politics students who were shadowing me for the day* came into the gallery of the chamber of the House of Commons as I was due to speak in a debate. During the debate, the Tory MP Alec Shelbrooke and I took absolute lumps out of each other, at times getting quite aggressive. After I had finished, I went out to the members' lobby to be reunited with the keen students and Alec Shelbrooke walked out of the chamber as I greeted them. He came over and said something along the lines of, 'Hi, Jess, how are you doing? Are we still on for the meeting later? I've got some interesting stuff I think might be useful.' We chatted, laughing and joking with each other for a minute, and agreed we would be meeting later. The students looked on aghast that two people who had just been trying to trip up the other were just minutes later chatting as if nothing had happened and were in fact in cahoots on an issue.

This is not to say that what happened in the Commons' chamber was fake or even affected for an audience (although a lot of it is) – I really did hate what he had been saying and wanted him to know that – but the truth is that on other

* On average, I would say I get around a hundred requests a year from individuals, schools, universities and charities from all over the country to ask if people can come to Parliament to shadow me and gain experience. I like to do as much of this as possible because I want to open up this world to as many people as I can; I would estimate that at least half of the time I spend in Westminster I am accompanied by someone shadowing me and my team.

issues I can work really well with him and I need members of the governing party to work with me to get shit done. I work with people whose views I loathe and detest all the time because that is how I get stuff done for the people that I care about. It is not possible for me to get laws changed, such as making domestic abuse refuges a legal duty, without having to charm the prime minister from time to time – this does not affect my ability to also criticise the actions the exact same prime minister is taking in other areas.

Many of my meetings will be cancelled at the last minute (sorry if I have ever done this to you) because of sudden changes to business that happen in the House of Commons. There might, for example, be an urgent question. Urgent questions can be on a variety of topics, ranging from 'The recent court order regarding the Government's publication of contracts during the COVID-19 pandemic' to 'The future of car manufacturing by Vauxhall at Ellesmere Port'. You do not know what these will be until around midday on a Monday so you might have three meetings that have been in your diary for months that have to be cancelled at the last minute if something of particular interest or relevance to you is raised.

Then we move on to the programmed business for the day, debating government legislation in the House of Commons or motions for debate put down by opposition parties. You only find out what will be discussed a few days in advance, at which point you have to decide whether or not to attend the session. I do not have to attend all of these (I would literally never get anything else done); debates are mostly attended by MPs particularly interested in the subject matter. If all MPs attended all debates we wouldn't even all fit in the chamber, which can only seat around 400 people (there are 650 of us). But if it is a debate on something that I have pushed for or an issue that affects my constituents* then the chances are that I will want to take part. This means all my meetings have to be cancelled while the business of Parliament takes precedence. You can see why managing my diary is a monumental pain in the arse.

Those meetings that aren't cancelled run a high risk of being interrupted. At the end of any debate, there is the potential for a vote or multiple votes to show the will of Parliament on the matter, which means summoning back all MPs who are off doing their business elsewhere. So you could very well be in the middle of a half-hour meeting that someone has waited months to have with you and the voting bell (we call it division bell) will ring continuously for eight minutes calling you to vote. This will usually take you around ten minutes but if there is more than one vote you won't be getting back to what you were doing for at least half an hour. This happens all the time and you can never really know throughout the day when the votes might occur, so you cannot plan for them.†

The worst occasion where I had to up and leave a meeting that I can recall was on the day of the Westminster terror attack in 2017. I had just sat down for a meeting with some-one from the Women's Budget Group when the division bell

---

* This is pretty much everything bar rural policy and fisheries. Don't get me wrong, they eat fish, they just don't have much skin in the game about the fishing industry what with being from the part of the country furthest from the sea.
† The one exception to this is on a Wednesday, which is usually allocated to opposition party debates, and the votes are fixed at 4 p.m. and 7 p.m.

rang. I rose from my chair in Portcullis House and promised to be back in ten minutes to continue the meeting, thankfully leaving my visitor with my colleague Sophie in the meantime. I ran down the escalators in Portcullis towards the older part of the estate to head to the voting lobbies. I heard some commotion and a bang from the streets outside but thought nothing of it and continued on my way. That bang was the sound of a car being crashed into a crowd of people on Westminster bridge.

Once we had voted, I went to make my way back to the meeting only to find that security had locked us all into the chamber and the lobbies. We were told there was 'an incident'. I tried to call Sophie but could not reach her. When I eventually did get hold of her she told me how she and my visitor had been told to run and hide by a stampede of people running through Portcullis House who had heard gunshots and were being told that there was an armed man in Parliament. It must have been terrifying. Sophie had hurried our guest back to our office and locked them in.

It was another six hours before I was released from the chamber of the Commons and our staff were told that they could safely come out of our offices. For hours and hours, the police were concerned that there would be a follow-up attack or that snipers might be positioned around Parliament. There are many worse things that happened that day but I really felt for the woman who came to see me, was interrupted by the voting bell after a matter of minutes and was then locked for hours in a tiny Westminster office without any food or drink. (She has since been in for many meetings which were more successful.)

This is a dramatic example of course, but a normal day in Parliament doesn't really exist — there is always something that comes up that will kybosh all of your plans. Sometimes it is as dramatic as a security incident; more usually it is an emerging national situation (such as the Grenfell Tower disaster or a major employer declaring bankruptcy) or a murder or a fire in your constituency. Or there might be a sudden revelation in the never-ending soap opera that is Westminster that needs responding to — say, a new harassment scandal or an MP being recorded as saying something obscenely racist, which will light up your phone with demands and requests from one of your team or from the media.

By 7 p.m. on a Monday, most of the meetings and the drama of the day have taken place and the journalists send off the copy for tomorrow's news. Usually this is the time when I meet with a crowd of my colleagues and go and get some dinner together. But because Parliament starts late on a Monday, it also finishes late. So nine times out of ten, you'll be back after dinner to vote on the debates of the day between 9 and 10 p.m. In which case, in the time between my dinner and the final vote, I will head back to my office, which has been vacated by my staff as I do not expect them to keep to the same ridiculous hours as me, and start to do some of the work that has come up in the course of the day. I will read the briefings I have been given and send out emails to my staff to delegate following up on various actions, such as putting in for an adjournment or backbench debate, or writing to ask for a meeting with the relevant minister. I also need to look over what is in my diary for the next day, do any reading in preparation for tomorrow's meeting and make a plan for any speeches I will make or questions I will be asking in the chamber. I do not really write out speeches in advance as I tend only to give speeches in the Commons on things I can speak about fluently and with authority,* but I do make a brief note of exactly what it is I am asking for and three points I might want to highlight within that.

At 9 p.m., I will ring my husband and ask to speak to my children before they go to bed. Nine o'clock used to be their bedtime but they are both teenagers now and bedtime is more of an abstract concept than a firm reality. If you were to listen in to the conversations you might wonder why I bother. They have nothing to say about their day at school, nothing to tell me about what they have been doing and they usually answer with a simple 'yes' or 'no' to my increasingly inane questions. When my children have been naughty and I am shouting at them, or if they want something, then they will play the card that they find it very hard that I live away from them. They will make a right old song and dance when they leave me on a Monday morning to go to school, asking me when I am coming home as if they cannot bear my departure – but you would never know this from our phone calls. I end up acting like a demented stalker, asking questions like, 'What did you have for your tea?' and 'Who did you sit next to at

---

* Alas, this is not a generally applied rule of thumb. Many MPs feel that they must be seen speaking about absolutely everything and so pipe up in many debates with very little beyond a well-known statistic on the subject and whatever has been sent to them in a briefing. Personally, I find this maddening because debate is meant to be more than just a list of facts and figures quoted from a briefing that everyone has already read. Some MPs are obsessed with being visible; some are genuine eccentrics who just love the chamber and the theatre of it. I only ever speak or ask a question if I have a solid outcome I am seeking and my speaking might make that outcome more likely.

lunchtime?' in a vain attempt to get anything more riveting from them that, 'Yeah, it was okay, Mom.' My children have grown used to a life of me being away, so nowadays they don't know any different and wonder why I make any sort of fuss. I blame their father – stupid, calm, supportive and resilient man that he is.

The 10 p.m. vote bell tolls and I put on my coat, grab my suitcase of clean clothes and head to the voting lobbies. On a Monday night, the lobbies resemble a wartime evacuation scene. MPs wrapped up in puffa jackets and scarves clutch their worldly possessions, ready to break out into the cold London night to walk back to their lodgings or hustle for a cab along the road lined with 200 other MPs ready to elbow each other out of the way. The grounds of Parliament are paved with cobbles, which plays absolute bloody havoc with a wheelie suitcase and makes a terrible din as the wheels rattle across. I have often thought it must be a killer for the women who wear heels to work – although maybe that is intentional, a sort of cattle grid to keep well-heeled women out.

As you walk through the lobby all wrapped up with your luggage in tow, you will pass one of your party whips who is there to tell you if there is another vote expected or if you can go home. Desperate MPs await the sound of the four best words ever uttered in Parliament: 'Thank you and goodnight.' This means you are free to leave. It is quite remarkable how a group of people who have been accomplished enough to rise up in their field of expertise then climb the political ranks, who have the toughness and resilience that it takes to get elected to the House of Commons, revert to school kids meekly waiting for permission to go. We are told that we must not leave the parliamentary estate until 10 p.m. and by and large we all capitulate. Of course, it is my job and I am paid well to do it but it is utter madness that at the end of a sixteen-hour day, in which I have travelled over a hundred miles, been in endless battles, debates and meetings, during which I have acted with authority, been firm and expected people to listen to me, here I am acting like a kid, expectantly looking up at the teacher with desperation in my eyes, hoping to be dismissed.

Every night as I walk out of Parliament, I pass MPs asking each other, 'Are we done for the day? Can we go home now?', never willing to believe it until they have had the nod from at least five people. The fear is that should we sneak out the school gate only for another vote to be called, we would be so publicly and privately shamed that we would never be able to show our faces in Westminster again. This is ridiculous, as I have missed votes before by accident and it made literally no material difference. But the place has such a phenomenal hold on the MPs; institutionalised doesn't come close to describing it. I can't help but think that this reverence, while charming, might in fact be a worry and one of the reasons why things seem to progress so slowly within Westminster's halls.

I leave Parliament and I head back to my flat in London. I don't own this flat; I rent it, and that rent comes under my expenses and is paid for by the taxpayer. I need to have a place to stay in London as there is no way I could finish work at 10 p.m., or often much later, then travel back to Birmingham, arriving at 1.30 a.m., only to get back on a train at 6.30 a.m. in order to be back in London for 9 a.m. and another working day. I don't like it any more than the average taxpayer does. I wish I could do my job and live in my house with my family, but I can't; it would simply be impossible.

I have often had Jeremy Corbyn's expenses (or lack thereof) thrown at me as a sign of his sheer virtue in not claiming anything for a flat or for travel as if this is out of the goodness of his heart. It isn't: he lives in and represents a constituency that is twenty-five minutes from Parliament. He doesn't need a place to stay because politics happens in the place he lives. I understand that people don't want us living in needless luxury at huge expense, and I agree with them, but if I didn't have my accommodation funded in the capital I simply could not afford to be an MP. Being an MP would then be a pursuit that was only available to very rich people who live in the south – which, let's face it, can already feel like the case, even when they do allow oiks like me to have a flat in Stockwell to kip in.

I head back to my flat and I go straight to bed. I don't sleep though; that would be another lie. This is the time that I take to my phone and catch up on the news of the day. It is amazing how, when you are working in the heart of current affairs, among the people who are writing and broadcasting the news, and often walking past the news as it is happening, accidentally appearing in the background of shots, you totally miss most of what is going on in the world outside the windows. For example, I totally missed all the news about Sir Tim Peak going to the space station in 2015 and had no idea who he was until he was back on Earth and doing the interview rounds on breakfast news. 'Who is this fella?' I asked my husband one Sunday morning as we watched the telly over a cup of tea. He looked at me, baffled, as if I was asking who the Queen was, and exclaimed, 'How have you missed the whole story of a Brit in the space station? It's been everywhere?!'

I miss a lot of things while I am at work, running from meeting to meeting, debate to debate and committee to committee, so at the end of the day, when the adrenaline is still pumping and keeping me from sleep, I make an effort to catch up on the comings and goings of the world. I lie in the dark, in a bed that will never feel like my bed, my face illuminated by the small screen, and read through the news and Twitter and catch up on a few messages. My day ends as it started, fretting about what the hell is going on and what I might have got wrong.

I can feel you, dear reader, nervously noting that you have already read thousands of words about what I do in a normal week and we are only at the end of Monday. Well, worry no more, because Tuesday and Wednesday are essentially Monday repeated. Debates, meetings, run-ins with journalists, votes and I'm done. Though there are a few small differences.

On a normal Tuesday, I'm in Westminster for 8.30, my meetings begin at 9, the proceedings of Parliament start at 11.30 a.m. instead of 2.30 p.m. and, as a rule, the voting starts at 7.00 p.m., so you can usually leave by 7.30ish. However, because we finish earlier, Tuesday evenings are considered to be the best night to hold events in and around Parliament in order to get MPs to attend – dinners, fundraisers and the like. I have an evening-wear top permanently hanging in my office so I can glide seamlessly from woman in work suit to woman in work suit with a slightly sparkly top. Unlike

Clark Kent's ability to entirely hide his identity as Superman by donning a pair of specs, my efforts at evening attire are wholly unconvincing. I am constantly saying, 'So sorry, I've just come from work' to tables full of people more dressed up than I was on my wedding day.

Most Tuesday evenings find me speaking, presenting, entertaining and being lobbied at an event with warm white wine and mini quiches. There are award ceremonies for every tiny little thing under the sun. Like me, many MPs and politically adjacent folks write books that must be launched. Many charities hold evening events to launch their new campaigns. Newspapers, magazines and the news media have awards ceremonies that require people to present. In the first year I was elected to Parliament, I survived entirely on a diet of canapes, never once cooking a meal in my flat. If I so wished, I could be at an event eating crudités every lunch and dinner time in Parliament. I give my Tuesday nights to such events because on Monday nights I have to work and on Wednesday nights I travel home to Birmingham. I'm quite happy to do so, as it's not as though I'm missing an evening with my family or my friends, who are all far away.

I am making myself sound very sad. I do of course have friends in London – in fact, my very best friend Alex lives in London – but the truth is that Parliament is largely too unreliable to make plans with them and I really tire of making arrangements to go out for dinner or to go to a mate's house only to have to send a message at 5 p.m. that reads, 'Sorry, looks like votes might run past 7 p.m. tonight and I won't be done until 9.' Westminster workdays are entirely unpredictable.

However, I do get to go to some really cool events and a lot of the time I can take one of my mates with me, so that is how I tend to socialise with my people in London. We go to awards of fancy women's magazines, or film premiers and special theatre shows. A lot of famous people are involved in various political causes so you might be at a dinner on media standards with Hugh Grant one evening and the next you are with Idris Elba launching a strategy for diversity in television.* It's not all minute-taking and emails about saving hen harriers.

Wednesday is as Tuesday was. The main difference is that when you arrive at the gates of Parliament gripping your coffee you are greeted by police vans with sniffer dogs and usually a growing queue of people waiting to go through security to come in to the public areas of the building. Wednesday is Parliament's big set-piece day where the prime minister will be questioned by MPs in the imaginatively named Prime Minister's Questions, or PMQs. The prime minister is in parliament far more often than just on a Wednesday – he votes in the lobby with us most evenings without anything like this level of security fanfare – but because so many of the public come in to PMQs and it is a big event, the dogs are sent to check out the chamber.

When I was first elected, I would try to get into the chamber of the House of Commons really early to get a good seat

---

* Idris Elba was really nervous giving a speech in Parliament and afterwards when we were all posing for a big group photo, I cracked a joke and made him laugh. He said to me, 'It's really helpful that you made me smile for the photo, I should take you to all these things with me so I can smile for the camera.' To which I replied, 'I gratefully accept your proposal of marriage.' I am in fact engaged to Idris Elba but we like to keep it private.

so I could be in among the atmosphere of PMQs. For a political geek like me, that feeling of taking your seat in your first PMQs, soaking up all the noise and hullabaloo, was magical. I had watched it on the television pretty much every week of my life. The chamber of the House of Commons is not big enough to fit all of us at once, so no matter how early you get there your bum may well be squeezed very tight by the time the prime minister rises to their feet to answer the first question. I thought I would never tire of it. I thought I would want to go each and every week. Well, my friends, I couldn't have been more wrong. I rarely attend PMQs anymore. I still usually watch it on television, like the old times, but now sat in my office while eating a sandwich and tweeting side-eye blazes at the lies and nonsense that the prime minister spouts. I have absolutely no interest in attending PMQs unless I have been selected in the lottery to ask a question myself. Maybe post-pandemic I will feel different.

During my early years in Parliament, I sat and watched Jeremy Corbyn taking on Theresa May and they were both woeful at PMQs. It does not make you a good prime minister or leader of the opposition to make PMQs entertaining and politically damaging to your opponent, although sadly this is what it has descended to. It has almost zero to do with how services are delivered or what decisions are made – it is political theatre and the principals just didn't have their hearts in it.

PMQs should be a time when the prime minister is grilled and given crucial scrutiny to ensure that he is doing the right thing. However, the current prime minister seems to be made of Teflon and any scrutiny bounces off him.

I wonder what would happen if my Wikipedia page read,

under 'number of children', 'at least six'. I fear that I wouldn't have made it to becoming an MP, let alone to prime minister. If one of my closest friends and principal staff members had given a press conference about going on a drive during a pandemic to 'test his eyes', it would never cross my mind that I could *not* sack that person. Anyway. A lot of my constituents want me to raise things at the weekly PMQ sessions and I would absolutely love to raise all their issues. I would love to read out the names of every disabled person who has been stripped of the money that they need to pay for care and all the elderly people who cannot access social care. I long to tell the prime minister about the woman I happened upon one Christmas who told me she had been waiting a week for someone to assess her care needs at home and how, at the age of ninety, she had been forced to go to the toilet in a bucket in her living room for over two weeks as she couldn't climb the stairs. I want desperately to look into the eyes of this man who cannot be arsed to comb his hair and tell him about the young girl in my constituency who has attempted to take her life following abuse at the hands of her father and then her peers, for whom I cannot get a referral to children's mental health services for a year. I want to tell him every single detail of the lives of the people where I live and I want him to hear it in front of the public.

But there are only so many questions you can ask. And instead I have to listen to some grovelling Tory MP desperate for a job stand up and use the one opportunity they will get this year to publicly put a question to the prime minister to ask something so baffling stupid it blows my mind. 'Would the prime minister agree to come to Derbyshire and sample the best pies in Britain with me, and will he join me in giving thanks to all working in the booming local pie industry?' Seriously, dude, I'm not asking you to be mean to your boss publicly, but can you at least ask a constructive question about something that you would like to see progressed in your constituency? Because this is just you and the prime minister standing in front of Parliament and the public having very unfunny rofl rofl bantz with each other.

After PMQs, we go into debates. On Wednesday, the opposition parties get to decide what is debated so it usually ends up with a lot of rowing over child poverty, unemployment, homelessness, Brexit, workers' rights, devolution issues and other such affairs. The opposition, to the best of my knowledge, has never tabled a motion for debate about pies, but no doubt in all the years of Parliament I could well be wrong.

Parliament does sit on a Thursday but I try to go home to Birmingham on a Wednesday night after votes between 7 and 8 p.m. We are rarely called to vote on a Thursday and most of the debates that take place are backbench business debates. I would stay for these if I felt I had something insightful to say that would help the matters resolve but mostly I want to get back to my life in the constituency.

Westminster is my Monday, Tuesday and Wednesday; as I arrive home at around 11 p.m. on Wednesday night I have already worked a nearly forty-hour week. I don't tell you all this for some sort of praise or rehabilitation of members of Parliament – as you can tell, I have scant regard for many of them. I don't think I deserve sympathy for how tiring my life can be; I consider myself lucky in so many respects and

I recognise that there are a lot of people who work considerably more hours for considerably less pay. I simply tell you this because it is the truth. Lots of people think that MPs sit around doing nothing all day, having rows with each other and not giving a toss about ordinary folk. Maybe some do but the vast majority of MPs I encounter don't. They work very hard under immense pressure and strain, captured by an institution that is unbending to their life, their family, their need to sleep. I don't think I should be praised for my job unless I do it well but I certainly don't think it's fair to hate me for my job, regardless of how well I do it.

Now to the constituency. On Thursday morning my Birmingham work week begins and that is a whole different kettle of much friendlier but at times distressing fish.

4

Home Ground: Back in the Constituency

'Dear Sir, I have read about you on the internet and see you are a very eminent leader of your blessed country. I am very good student and wish to work in your country. Please find attached a copy of my CV and I would graciously like to ask you to sponsor my entry into the country and send me a letter of recommendation so I can come to Great Britain.'

I'll ignore for a second that even the most basic research on the internet would identify that I am not a sir (and not just because I have never kneeled in front of the Queen; I have other barriers to contend with in that area). Members of Parliament receive letters like this every couple of months. It is just one very stark example of the wild expectations people have regarding the power held by British members of Parliament.

For the avoidance of doubt, being a member of Parliament does not sign you up to a Tinder-style portal where you can swipe right for the folks you think should be given a British passport and bin the ones who appear in clearly curated pictures where they are pretending they don't realise the picture is being taken and are looking thoughtfully into the distance (why do people do this?). No thank you, wistful-looking posing charlatan.

Similarly, I do not have a drawer in my office full of keys to empty council properties, ready to hand out when people want to move. Sadly, I don't even have the power to find homes for those in real need, perhaps facing abuse and homelessness. I do not have a school place for your child in the exact school you wish to send them to halfway through the academic year. If you are sixteenth on a school waiting list because you moved to a new house in December, no letters from me to said school will mean that they kick out another kid so that your child can fill their place. I once asked an anxious parent, 'Do you understand that what you are asking the school to do is walk into a classroom, pick a child at random and send them home with a letter that says, "Sorry, your child can no longer attend our school because someone else wanted your child's place really badly"?' To my astonishment, the parent in question seemed fine with that and asked me to get on with it.

I cannot compel the court to overturn your conviction, I cannot demand that your electricity bill be immediately reduced. I do not have the ability to stop the leaves falling from the trees outside your home, nor can I control the weather. And yet, I have been asked to do all these things. People often have wild expectations of what I can achieve. I *might* – and I would like to stress *might* in the strongest terms here – be able to get your missed bin collection sorted. Oh, the power. A constituent once came to see me to complain about their neighbour's overflowing skip, which had been left on the drive for months and months, demanding that I raise the issue in Parliament and, more specifically, that I take it to the prime minster.

The truth is that as said skip was not doing anything illegal, even the prime minister himself, the first lord of the Treasury and de facto commander in chief of the British armed forces, can do naff all to get the people at number 45 Orchard Road, Yardley, to move their skip if they don't want to. I guess he could change the law about the time limits on skips but even that would take a couple of months to do and I'm thinking that he probably has more pressing legislation he wants changing.

People often stop me in the street to tell me things that I should say to Boris Johnson; my dad rings me on a thrice-daily basis with helpful suggestions of what to tell the prime minister. I wish all MPs had one hour a week to sit in front of the prime minister and run through what Janet from Acocks Green thinks of the common agricultural policy or to give him a piece of my father's mind on this week's performance by the Health Secretary on *Question Time*; alas, it's simply not an option. On a few occasions when I have seen the PM around, I have just walked up to him and started regaling him with these opinions, along with some of my own. He usually just looks desperate to get away and, on one occasion, started telling me about how we needed to 'get Brexit done', which was weird because I wasn't talking to him about anything to do with the UK's relations with the European Union. After that, I did come to suspect that he has a pull cord in his back, like Woody from *Toy Story*, which just delivers one of a random selection of slogans if he is ever approached by a member of the public or an opposition MP. Odd chap.

So I've clarified that I can't get you a house, a school place or a visa, and I can't get the annoying skip removed from the drive of that toerag next door, and I can't take up every issue that you have directly with the prime minister; I guess a fair question would be, other than getting your bin emptied, what *can* I do?

While I do not have any power to unilaterally change anything, what I do have is the will, skills, practice and platform to try to change anything. The job of an MP is to advocate on behalf of one's constituents. That can be as simple as firing off an email to the council to ask them to collect the bloody bins right up to finding a case of wrongdoing so awful and unfair in your own backyard that you undertake years of research and run a campaign over a decade to try to change the law so that it can never happen again. This happens much more than you might think; in fact, most new legislation in this country comes from an initial meeting between a constituency MP and someone who has been wronged or failed by the perceived wisdom of the system.

On the day I am writing this it is a Sunday and it is very sunny outside. I have just returned home from an unremarkable semi-detached house in my constituency where I sat for an hour with a woman who we'll call Annie. Annie is only nine years older than me, however she is so shrunken and crippled by the challenges she has faced that she looked a hundred years old. I received a call on the preceding Friday from her son, who told me that Annie had suffered such a terrible seizure due to alcohol withdrawal that she'd had to be hospitalised. She was now trying to discharge herself and her son didn't know what to do because he didn't feel that they could cope with looking after her at home but there was nowhere else for him to turn. He gave me the number for his nan and told me that she was a retired nurse and might explain things better. I spoke to Annie's mom, who explained that she was caring for her own ninety-year-old mother as well as for her brother, who had just come out of hospital and was staying with them (honestly some people get all the luck – and by 'some people' I mean women), and she needed help and advice for her daughter, who suffered from alcoholism, anorexia and osteoporosis.

The first thing I will do in a case like this is deal with the immediate options. Like Sherlock Holmes, I will plug into my mind palace, which is aided by an online caseworker system, and I will file through the similar cases I have dealt with in the past, looking at what has worked and what hasn't. Which facilities are available to me? What are the barriers to access? (I could pretend otherwise but the answer to this last one is almost exclusively money; if you have cash then barriers are easier to vault.) I will think about who else I can go to for advice and who will be able to find out quickly if there is a place for Annie to go – a bed, a service, a group, anything. It is at this moment that you start to run into the politics of the situation. Up until this point, it had been a completely human issue: my responsibility had been to speak in calming, steady and trustworthy tones; there was no need for a rosette or campaign slogans, just ears and heart. The politics enters when you start to see how policy decisions made by governments can help or hinder people in Annie's situation. I am afraid to say that, at the moment, it is usually more hinder than help.

I found a rehab bed Annie could go to but the first barrier is that it cost £10,000. Not an option; strike it off the list. I found another local facility where there was a slim chance – but a chance, nonetheless – that I could get a mixture of charity and state funding to cover the cost. Hooray, a ray of sunshine crept in. But I called and of course there was no room at the inn. So now I had no palatable options for this family; it was going to require some compromise about how far she may have to travel for help, how much money they can spare and what they are expecting.

Before I spent hours that will turn into weeks on the case, I decided that first I needed to speak to Annie directly and assess for myself whether this was what *she* wants. I don't mean to sound harsh but there are around 110,000 people in my constituency and on this particular Friday, at least a hundred of them had been in touch with me about something they needed help with. Also, speaking to Annie was the right and ethical thing to do – she is a fully grown woman. I asked to see her the next day and she agreed, which is a real positive and was by no means a guarantee. At this stage, a spanner was thrown in the works because on the Saturday I was due to see her, my own elderly father took an almighty tumble in his garden and I ended up with him, some very patient paramedics and a six-hour stretch in A&E. I put Annie off until the next day and promise I will make my best efforts to see her the next morning.

On arrival at Annie's house, I was greeted by a dog big and enthusiastic enough to nearly knock me off my feet. As we were in the middle of a global pandemic, I felt a little nervous going into the house and had to make sure I kept two metres away from the people there. I always found this very hard, as my experience is that in difficult situations with vulnerable people, being as familiar as possible and, where appropriate, being tactile can help people feel at ease – especially if they expect you to be a bit of a stuck-up stuffed shirt (to be fair, none of my constituents think this of me; some of them hate me and think I am useless and stupid, but 'reserved' and 'stuffy' are charges I have never faced).

I sat down in the garden in the burning morning sun with this tiny woman, smaller than either of my children, and I talked to her about her life. I had never met her before and she told me things she hadn't told anyone in years. Sad things. I listened. This is the greatest gift of having the letters MP after my name: no matter how much people revile untrustworthy MPs and slag us off when stopped by a television interviewer on the street, it often puts you in a position where people trust you to handle their lives. This gift should be leaned on but never exploited.

The other gift you get, and this one is far less deserved, is that people often assume you know what the hell you are talking about on literally every single subject in the world. I should caveat this: I'm talking about people who *perceive* themselves to be lower in the unwritten pecking order than you. People who, usually for class reasons, think that those who have been elected to office have some sort of superior power and must be better at things than they are. People often think that I know every single law and regulation; I don't. People have assumed I am an expert on everything from the US–China trade wars to the United Kingdom fisheries policy. I know nothing about either, literally nothing, and, just like you would, I'd probably start with Wikipedia if I had to find out about them. In some situations (Donald Trump), this a terrifying danger of our politics. However, it also enables you to proffer valuable advice with authority and people will trust you. I find that often I am giving the exact same advice as someone's family and friends, but due to my position it is more respected.

Luckily for Annie, I am an expert by experience, practice and research in the problems that she is facing. So I could firmly but kindly tell her what her options were and what I thought would be best for her and her family, and she would hear me.

So now I will go away and I will advocate on her behalf, initially to deal with her immediate needs, which will involve trying to get her a place in a facility that can help her, and then looking into an ongoing support system. I will seek funding for her place and try to get the many ducks in a row so that she and her family can start to swim down the stream by themselves.

I hope that Annie will not need my help beyond that point. And yet, this is just the beginning for me. Annie's case will transfer into a different, wider part of my job – the part that tries to ensure that people like Annie's son don't need to panic and look around for a person with a higher status to look after them when something goes wrong.

When people come to me it is because the system has failed and it is my job not just to iron out the individual crease but to invent a new wrinkle-free material. Leading on from the case of Annie, her son and her mother, I will advocate for better carers' rights and security. I will research national spending patterns on substance misuse services for women. I will look at how funding for rehab facilities and support charities has changed over the years and I will fight to make it better in the future.

I won't do any of this on my own. I am not superhuman; I have staff and facilities available to me. I will seek the advice of experts and specialists, because my job opens doors, and together we will find a fix and then fight for it to be implemented. To be quite honest, much of this will fall on deaf ears and I don't have the power to *make* it happen. But I do have reasonable expectations of what I can do and, as I am constantly trying to explain to my constituents who think I have the power of Grayskull, all I can do is try.

When you are a member of Parliament you have at least three specific and distinct jobs. These are Westminster legislator, constituency social worker and political activist. If you are a liberally minded woman, you inevitably have to add feminist activist to that roster as well; similarly, if you possess any of the protected characteristics of the 2010 Equality Act, you will be expected to fight for those groups by virtue of your identity. I think this is potentially a chore – many people, for example, don't want to be 'a Jewish MP' or 'a disabled MP' – but luckily I am more than happy to add 'feminist warrior' to my ordinary working practices. One man's feminazi zealot is another woman's freedom fighter.

If you are any good at your job of being a representative of the people, you will link every single part of your job back to the social work element. You will root the legislation you wish to change or develop, or any political activism you undertake, in the life experiences of the people who sent you to the palace. Even when discussing issues of foreign affairs or international development, I think about the experiences of my constituents and their families at home and abroad. I realise that representing a constituency that could boast of having a resident from pretty much every country in the world makes this easier for me. Even without this, however, it shouldn't be too much of a stretch to see how war and disorder in a far-off land such as Syria threatens the security of our constituents and will have a direct effect on services that they might use. You don't have to represent Syrian refugees to be able to see that a war in Syria is a threat in our own constituencies.

It is for this reason that it is my very strong belief – I would go so far as to say it is a fact – that politicians who are most in touch with the people that they represent, who do the most work in their communities, who have a constant link between themselves and their constituents, are better politicians. In the far-gone past, before high-speed rail and internet communications, the convention was for politicians to visit their constituencies sparingly. I remember when I was first elected, a very eminent and senior politician, who now has a seat in the House of Lords, asked me to meet her for a cup of tea.* This grand dame looked aghast when I said that I lived, worked, shopped and educated my children among my constituents. 'Familiarity breeds contempt, my dear!

---

* New and junior MPs meeting senior figures for a cup of tea in one of the many tearooms in Parliament is the most Parliament thing to do. I have eaten a lot of scones in my time and it is probably one of the reasons that, according to the folklore, new MPs put on at least a stone when first elected.

In my day we just visited perhaps once a month for a town hall meeting.'

To be honest, there are times when this level of familiarity can be a challenge. During the Brexit votes in Parliament, I couldn't whip around the local Asda without having to go into some detail with a fellow shopper about taking back control and which laws do and don't get made in Europe, or having to counsel people in the cleaning aisle about how it was all going to end. Sometimes I just wanted to buy a bunch of bananas without having to discuss whether the European Union had or hadn't made demands on how bendy said fruit was permitted to be.* I have to say, in 2020, the mask-wearing brought about by the Covid-19 global pandemic coupled with a dramatic lockdown haircut made popping to get a pint of milk a considerably quicker exercise.

But of course I jest because in reality I want to be as close as possible to my constituents. I want to feel their lives happening around me and I need to understand what is helping them to progress and what is holding them back. In the United Kingdom, we take for granted the closeness between an elected representative and their electorate. The fact that politicians of all hues make time each month to meet with constituents in an advice surgery, and we spend our weekends knocking on their doors even when there isn't an election on the horizon, is pretty much unique. It's certainly very different from how political representatives behave in most other parts of the world.

---

* For the record, the European Union never said bananas couldn't be bendy. This was a lie manufactured by idiots. They literally don't give a toss how bendy our fruit is.

One cold but bright Saturday morning, I headed out for a street surgery (knocking doors and asking people for their issues) with a team of volunteers in Yardley. A new volunteer had come along to help. Originally from Cameroon, this man was new to my constituency but he had joined the Labour Party and wanted to come along and meet me out doing my job. I explained the process to him, that we would go to each house on the street, he should introduce himself as a volunteer for the local Labour Party and ask if the residents had any concerns that they wished to raise with their local MP. I suggested he join me for the first few doors so he could get the hang of it before going alone. He looked totally baffled and asked me to clarify. 'You are going to knock on the doors of these people?' 'Yep, I do it most weeks and have been doing this kind of thing since before I could walk.' He could not believe that an elected member of the UK Parliament would engage with the people like this. 'Where I come from elected officials would only drive past in cars with blacked-out windows.'

My French sister-in-law is a civil servant in the north of France who deals with elected politicians all the time. She was similarly dumbfounded when she overheard me one Sunday morning on the phone to a constituent who was complaining that the leaves that had fallen on the pavement outside her house had not been cleaned up by the council. She joked with my brother, 'Can you imagine if we tried to call our *député* because there were leaves outside our house?' She was amused by this thought for a solid twenty minutes.

According to one of the stories that get passed around Parliament, when William Hague was the Foreign Secretary, at meetings such as the G20 summit, his foreign counterparts would ask him to tell funny stories from his surgeries with constituents. The then-Secretary of State under President Obama, Hillary Rodham Clinton, would allegedly lead the other global leaders of foreign affairs in their merriment – 'William, tell us the stories about your advice sessions.' With the possible exception of Ireland, the United Kingdom is probably the only country in the world where you could expect the prime minister, the first lord of the Treasury, to sit in a draughty church hall every other Friday night to listen to people complaining about their next-door neighbour playing music too loud.

It may well be the butt of a joke at the G20 summit that British politicians are expected to maintain a link with the lives of the electorate, but it is without question the very best part of my job. If I did not have Thursday, Friday and Saturday mornings with my constituents, I would genuinely give up being a member of Parliament. They are my sanity. They are often the light moments of comedic glory in a week where you might have had to sift through thousands of legislative words about the minimum sentencing for rape or had people threatening to kill you because of your political views. When leaving my family home on a Monday morning to travel over a hundred miles to take part in hours of votes into the late evening, the result of which were already decided before I woke up in the morning because votes are so whipped, I often think, 'What am I doing this for?' Then, every Thursday, when my constituency office opens its doors and in file five or six constituents, I am back where I belong and it is easy to answer this question. I keep going for them because it is a privilege to be invited into their lives – no matter how ridiculous some of their requests might be.

Let's deal with the ridiculous. I am an elected representative of the people. I am not a postman, I do not do domestic odd jobs, I am not an expert in domestic insects. Nor am I a search engine. If someone were to pull the string on my back, *Toy-Story*-Boris-Johnson-style, my catchphrase would be: 'Let me Google that for you.' It would appear that a lot of people think my office is a sort of directory enquiries. Requests such as 'Do you know what time the post office opens on a Saturday?' or 'What date will the Christmas market open in the city centre this year?' are among some of the easiest cases I have to deal with. 'Let me Google that for you.' Never once has anyone said in response, 'I guess I could have done that myself.'

I really don't mind this kind of interaction with my constituents. Where I live, almost all advice services, community centres and local council offices have been closed down, thanks to years of austerity, and so I think in most cases what people actually want is someone to talk to, a human interaction. I am happy to be that person; I only ask that they understand that while my team and I are Googling things for them, we are probably also handling a case where a constituent could be facing a death sentence in a Saudi Arabian courtroom, or a family has just been turfed out of their home and is facing a night on the streets. Let me Google that for you – but could it wait just five minutes?

One woman rang my office to ask if we could help her shift some unwanted paving slabs. They were her slabs, left at the bottom of her private garden. I tried to explain that we were not a domestic odd-job service and we attempted to refer her to a local paid service who could do it but she said she couldn't afford it. Politicians must tread a fine line of expectation management with their constituents, not least because if you do something for one person, word can get around. It is vital that people understand the parameters of both my job and my capabilities and very often we must spell this out pretty sternly. However, on this occasion, the woman had asked for help so many times I just gave in and my husband and his van went over and got rid of the slabs for her. It turns out I am an odd-job woman in that I do have a very odd job.

There are many instances like this when you know where the line is but, when it comes down to it, you are not just an MP, you are also a human being, and if you can help someone shift some slabs then why not just do it. Not least because there are, of course, requests I can't help with. It is heartbreaking when someone comes in and tells you that they cannot afford to heat their home until the following week or that they don't have the cash to get themselves to college or work the next day. For many reasons, both practical and ethical, I cannot be handing out cash to people or paying their bills.*

What I can do is use my platform to ask for help, so I will take to Twitter or send out an email to my contacts and ask

---

* There are rules in law which disallow the 'treating' of the electorate, which means essentially the giving of gifts or money to constituents. This is forbidden for the obvious reason that rich people could just buy themselves popularity. Though this is a standard practice in many countries around the world and in certain instances I have had to explain to my constituents who come from a country that practises treating that we don't give out houses or cash here.

for volunteer donations (of money or time) to help someone out. I have over the years been able to build up a welfare kitty so that when someone needs it, I can pop over the road to the shops and get them a bag of food or a packet of nappies. I can put a bit of money on your electric card or buy you a week's travel pass so you can get the bus, or I can rally a few people to come and clear your garden.

I remember on one occasion, a woman who had fled domestic violence had come in for support; we'd eventually managed to get her a council home and set her up safely, only for a fire to decimate that home just a few weeks later, leaving her with no furniture or home comforts. You'd like to think that there would be some local resource I could tap into to solve this problem but I am afraid there just isn't, so I took to Twitter to ask for help. Within a few hours, we had sofas, dining tables, TVs and more plates and cutlery than we could cope with.

Similarly, every year without fail, there will be families in Yardley who cannot afford the basics at Christmas, so we put out a call and parcels arrive from all over the country, containing Lego sets, beautiful illustrated books and fresh new pyjamas. Father Christmas definitely exists in Birmingham Yardley.

The vast majority of people who make these sorts of practical requests of me are asking because they remember a time when going to your MP was the approved course of action for these things. A time when there was a local charitable or council garden clearance service, when there was a specific welfare fund they could tap into in order to meet their immediate needs. I am afraid all of that is gone now and I often have to sit in front of constituents and explain that a decade of cuts to local services and a prevailing ideology that an individual should be completely in charge of their own destiny, as if outside influences play no part, means that I have nowhere to send them. Lots of people accept this explanation but some will huff that the previous member of Parliament would have done it – which of course is true, because the previous member of Parliament worked under a government who made sure these services were provided. A constituent once told me that the previous member of Parliament had always collected his bins – as if the MP was himself the bin man. He wasn't, he just took credit for a well-funded and -run council service that had naff all to do with him.

There are of course some things that I simply cannot deliver. On one occasion, a woman brought a spider in a jar into my office. She claimed that this was a false widow spider and she wanted me to find the antidote to its bite. Now, I am no zoologist, but to me it just looked like a house spider, and even if it wasn't I would not be the person to come to, not least because my office is sadly lacking in the lab equipment to work on such things. Which seems reasonable, as this is the first and only time that the bite of the false widow spider has been of pressing concern to my constituents. I gave her the number for the RSPCA, although I'm pretty sure protecting this animal was not at the top of her list of priorities.

Some members of Parliament have very strict protocols about what they do and don't deal with. Some won't deal with requests that are about council services as that is an entirely different political structure. Some simply don't handle cases of immigration on principle; one MP even said to me, 'There

are no votes in immigration case work, why do you bother?'
The answer is that I don't really like my constituents being
wrongfully held in immigration detention* and I think it is
perfectly acceptable for someone's elderly mother to want to
come and visit them, just as I might wish to visit a member
of my own family living abroad. I also think it is possible to
fall in love with someone from another country. I am such a
modern Millie.

There is a hard-and-fast rule in Parliament that you don't
take cases from outside your area. This is a sensible rule; I
cannot be the caseworker for the whole nation and what the
hell do I know about children's services in Wiltshire? And
yet I find this rule almost impossible to live by because some
people have really crap MPs who have done nothing at all
to help them when they legitimately need it. Lots of people
get in touch and say that their Tory MP won't help them
and many women contact me because they want to talk to a
woman about their issue not a man. This is a nearly impossible situation because MPs like me cannot be dealing with
a national level of casework when we are having to ask our
own constituents to wait at least two weeks for a response.

Another no-go area for MPs is the justice system in our
country. We do not live in America where many judicial roles
are elected – here in the UK, the judiciary and Parliament

---

* A constituent of mine who was working in this country completely legally,
as a civil servant for the Department for Justice in fact, was once detained
and threatened with deportation because he had made an error by under-
declaring his tax liability on his tax return. They said it showed bad character
and broke the conditions of his immigration status. He had under-declared
by £1.12. The same year, Jeremy Hunt, the Secretary of State for Health,
forgot to declare to Parliament that he had bought seven luxury apartments.
I'll wager that was more than £1.12.

are completely independent of each other. We make the laws; they test and practise them. I am forbidden to give out legal advice – firstly because I am not lawyer and secondly because members of Parliament are simply not allowed to do so. All I can do is seek the professional legal advice that you need. I can point out irregularities in how court proceedings may have played out; I can ask for a sentence to be made longer in certain circumstances, as can you;* I can give evidence in your case (which I do in lots of disability benefits tribunals and family law cases) but I do not sit above the judiciary and I cannot overrule the practice of law. And I certainly can't overturn a criminal conviction or undo a heavy sentence. This has disappointed many people who think I can.

On one occasion I was accused by a judge of being over-familiar with my constituents in the evidence that they presented in court. This constituent had been coming to see me for around a year about several difficult issues in her life. Like lots of my constituents, she had had her disability bene-fits terminated and was going through the long and arduous process of asking for this decision to be reviewed. The process is first dealt with by the Department for Work and Pensions and then, if that fails, it will, in many cases, end up in front of a tribunal hearing in court. This process involves people with terminal illnesses or lifelong disabilities having to prove

---

* Anyone can do this, not just MPs. Every citizen in this country has the right to write to the Attorney General and ask for some cases such as murder and manslaughter to be reviewed if they think the sentence is too lenient. You don't have to be connected to the case, you might just have read about it in the paper. I have done this with mixed success. Only lawyers and the accused, on the other hand, can seek to *reduce* a sentence through appeal in a court of law.

if they can work or not by undertaking a series of interviews about whether they can butter bread. It is a nonsense and in almost all the cases I have handled, the decision of the Department for Work and Pensions is overturned by the courts. The amount that this is costing our country is a scandal and you and I, the taxpayers, are paying for this process.

It is not uncommon for the evidence presented to the court to include correspondence with me, the local MP. This correspondence is often used as evidence for the difficulties that they have faced and on occasion I am also asked to give my professional opinion as to their well-being. I will give evidence such as: 'Mrs X has been seeking support from my office for X months/years regarding issues of her mobility and how that is affecting her housing situation. On every occasion that I have seen Mrs X, she has had to be supported by Mr X her carer and I can attest that in my opinion she could not cope without the care of another person.' I will only ever write what I know to be true and what I have witnessed.

On this occasion, the evidence presented was correspondence between me and this constituent, which was being used to show the kind of support she was requesting and how long she had been seeking this support from me. The judge in this case, however, ruled my evidence out of order. Not because of anything I had said in my statement, not because the correspondence did not back up my constituent's version of events, but because I had signed off one of my emails adding an 'x'. The judge said: 'Both the familiarity of the wording and the fact Ms Phillips places a kiss after her name, indicate a relationship of affection and friendship which goes beyond the parameters of a merely professional relationship.

In evaluating the contents of her email, we did so on the basis that Ms Phillips was writing as a friend rather than in a professional capacity.' The years that I spent climbing up the political pole, the thousands of disability benefit cases I have managed, the letters before and after my name were all snapped away in a heartbeat because I don't talk to my constituents like a robot.

Yes, I was familiar with her. I had been working on various cases with her and other members of her family for over a year. It was a complicated situation but one of the issues that this woman faced was her nervousness around figures of authority because of some pretty crappy things that had happened to her. It took some considerable bloody skill and patience to persuade this woman and her family to trust me, an establishment figure. My familiarity with her was a tool in order to help her. But aside from that, I accidentally put a kiss at the end of messages to everyone. There's no bloody law against it. I am fairly sure that if you dug around in my sent box you could find an email to the taxman that I signed off with a kiss. I often write emails on my phone where, thanks to years of text messaging, the kiss slips by. Anyway, the world needs more kisses.

This speaks to everything that is wrong with our political institutions when people think that being kind or familiar is somehow unprofessional. Okay, I don't expect court judges to be high-fiving the defendant or stopping to give a witness a cuddle, but to undermine my evidence because I was kind and compassionate to someone who needed help is quite something. I tell this story not to make me sound like an amazing loving MP (well, maybe a bit), but because I think it demonstrates the dual roles you have to somehow perform as a member of Parliament.

I am not sure exactly when it happened, but the addition of 'social worker' to an MP's job description is relatively new in the history of the role, and perhaps that balance hasn't yet worked itself out. It is hard to be both an approachable support worker for your constituents, many of whom are in dire and frightening situations, and at the same time a professional legislator who meets with senior court judges in fancy offices in Whitehall to talk about which laws need to change. On a Monday morning, I could be in front of a constituent with severe mental health needs who is threatening to take their own life and by that evening I am eating dinner off a silver platter in the American Embassy talking about British–US relations with the US ambassador. All in one day. I must be down home with my fellow Brummies and an equal sparring partner to the prime minister.*

I have frequently been told I am too emotional, and a minister once accused me of being led by my heart not my head in relation to some proposed amendments to the Domestic Abuse Bill. Er, both my head and my heart think that refusing a woman a refuge bed because she wasn't born in the UK is a shitty thing to do, and if your head disagrees then enjoy watching the murder rate rising and violent criminals being left to commit crimes with impunity. Some people have heads I can't understand. I have also been told that I practise student politics or that I am shroud-waving about the sad cases that

---

* Granted, at the moment I can safely say that any one of my constituents – even those searching for the cure for the venomous spider – would not struggle to outsmart the prime minister.

I see in my constituency work. It appears that I am meant to somehow compartmentalise the people I see and meet in my constituency and the job I do in Westminster, and I find that to be basically impossible.

Most members of Parliament treat their constituents' lives as the heartbeat of all that they do. However, when people rise to government there must be some sort of Faraday cage around their Whitehall offices that blocks out all messages about the realities of people's lives while the minister becomes totally obsessed with maintaining their position. I feel that I take to Twitter almost weekly to exclaim with total exasperation that ministers should come and spend just one day in my office listening to my constituents, because they seem so very unaware of their lives. This problem is definitely exacerbated by the political system we have, where the vast majority of people in cities (where immigration, deprivation, need for social housing and crime are at the highest) are represented by one political party (Labour) and people in towns and countryside are represented by the opposite side. I have absolutely no doubt that the ministers I have to face when talking about child poverty, degraded social housing and food poverty do not see even a tiny fraction of this in their own backyards. Equally, what the hell do I know about the rural economy?

This is not to say that my constituents are always right; they are not. It is common for new MPs to feel that they cannot say no to any request from their constituents, but you learn pretty quickly. I am no stranger to telling my constituents that I will not handle their cases for a huge host of reasons. I have even had to ban some from returning to my office because they have been racist or abusive to me or my staff.

On one occasion, a man came to my office to ask for help with the immigration process for his wife and young child. He was British and earned above the threshold for the rules to be met.* I said it would be very straightforward and that he should require very little help. However, when I delved into his refusal letter from the Home Office, it transpired that he already had a wife in the UK. I explained that you cannot legally have two wives and that there was no way that this could be overturned without a divorce. He looked at me as if I was unfeeling and told me that his current wife in the UK was ill and could no longer act as his wife and what did I expect him to do in these circumstances? As firmly and calmly as I could, I said, 'I expect you to look after her and not go off and marry someone else.' I mean, call me old-fashioned . . .

But for the most part, while I cannot promise that I can provide what my constituents need, I can promise that I will try. For many people, the act of coming to speak to an MP is undertaken because they have tried every other angle possible and they feel as if no one is listening to them. The very fact that these people keep going and keep trying is inspiring to me. People often ask me, how do you keep hopeful while handing out an ever-increasing number of food parcels or supporting someone who has been abused and gets no justice? How do you cope dealing with hundreds of families every week who are living in grubby hotels or people living on the streets?

The answer is that every single destitute or desperate

---

* In the UK, at time of writing, if you wish to bring over a spouse from another country you must prove that you earn at least £18,600 in order to satisfy the immigration service that you can support your partner.

person who comes to see me to ask me to take on their case does it because they are still hopeful something can change. They haven't given up on the possibility that things will come right. Many MPs and ex-MPs moan about how the job has changed beyond recognition because of the amount of constituency casework that now has to be done, but for me, no matter how funny it is to Hillary Clinton or my French sister-in-law, the fact that we have a political system where people have a right to be heard is a thing of sheer democratic beauty. In the UK, your case, your life could change the law forever, and that's really something.

5

The Power to Change:
How to Get Things Done

We live in an age where everyone is looking for a binary, looking for the quickest, snappiest tweet to express a complex issue. We act as though good vs evil is a thing. It isn't – not in politics, anyway.

I learned this lesson fairly early on in my career when the then prime minister David Cameron asked Parliament to vote on sending military air support (this is the politically palatable way of saying 'planes with bombs on them') to Syria. It was framed as a military intervention to help the rebel forces on the ground in the region to push back ISIS forces. Prior to the vote, the government laid on meetings where politicians could discuss with the leaders in the armed forces exactly what the plan was. We looked over maps, heard about tactics on the ground and expectations for other allies' military and diplomatic efforts. We were told that our support would allow local forces on the ground to join up and take back the regions ISIS had captured.

Obviously, I am no fan of ISIS. I have sat with Yazidi women and listened as they wept about their sexual enslavement by ISIS forces in the Middle East. I have heard of the horrors of young people groomed to fight for a cause that is not theirs. I have watched the trickle of blood as it spread across the ground from the brave police officer killed in Parliament by a man purporting to follow these extremists. They would absolutely kill me if they got the chance. I would do anything I could to eradicate the harm they seek to cause. So, I should vote for the bombs on planes, right? Well, yes, perhaps. But I didn't vote for the bombs on planes.

I didn't vote for it because I was not convinced by the plan that was laid out to me; I was not convinced that the disparate ground troops from differing regions and groupings in Syria just needed some British bombs – which could kill many innocent civilians in the process. If I had been surer of the plan and more certain it would work, I would have voted for the bombs on planes.

In the lead-up to the vote, I received hundreds of emails begging me not to vote for the bombing, and when I didn't, I was lauded by those same people for not agreeing to sacrifice the lives of civilians. But the case was being presented as if *all* military intervention is bad: the goodies would vote against bombs and the baddies would vote for them. This was wrong. The people who did vote for it were not baddies who love bombing countries; they believed that, in this case, the intervention would be a force for good. To suggest that people who vote for military intervention don't care about civilians on the ground is wrong – it's too basic, too binary.

Politicians do not take these votes lightly. For me, it felt like a harrowing decision and I spent weeks studying and considering my vote. (Though some people who had watched ten minutes of the news told me that the decision was bloody obvious.) But in this case, as in many others, there was no right or wrong answer. Every single outcome meant someone would suffer: doing something could kill people and doing nothing would mean people died. Frontline politics is not a game. I don't get to pick from two perfect options, or even two good options; I have to pick the least bad, which is tough when you go into politics bursting with idealism about changing the world for the better. It is not nice and it is not comfortable but I have to decide on a hierarchy of harms and the only way I know how to do that is to keep my focus on the potential outcome.

The Syria issue is far more complex than I can lay out here, but should we, in a different country, have intervened? I think so. It is too easy to say that it is none of our business, while millions die. What is more wrong is to say that it is none of our business and then to complain about the number of Syrian refuges coming to our shores. What did we think was going to happen?

I represent a good number of Syrian refugees who live in my constituency. One family come to mind, where the dad ran a thriving business in Damascus and the daughter was a specialist heart surgery scrub nurse. Now living in the UK, he is unemployed and she works in a local petrol station to support her family. I gave a school award to another Syrian boy for his brilliant achievements; this boy had watched his parents killed in front of him and his brother drown on the journey to find a new home. These people didn't want to come here, they didn't choose this life. I have asked many Syrian refugees who fled Assad's regime how they feel about the fact that the UK and the US did little or nothing in the way of intervention and the response is usually the same: they talk about how grateful they are to be here in the UK and how much they want to contribute to our country, but then they pose a question: 'If your city was on fire and your family were dying, wouldn't you hope someone would come to save you?'

Inaction in politics is not always a moral move. The job is not about what feels right, it is about trying to be a bit more right than you are wrong. A good outcome for the greatest number of people has to be realistic and likely before you can sign up to anything that will cause harm. If you enter politics already knowing that you would never vote for a bomb strike or that you would never agree to cut a certain service for the sake of a different one, then you are not cut out for the realities of political office. When a decision is made, when a law is passed or changed, some people will be harmed; my job is to make sure those 'some people' aren't always the *same* people.

Being an idealistic lefty and a proud socialist, born and bred, I believe we should share our nation's and our global wealth. But at the same time, we are nowhere near to equally sharing our nation's sacrifices, and perhaps that would be a good place to start. Why is it always the poorest, the blackest, the female, who take the hit first? Why did more Black and Asian people die in the UK of coronavirus? Why did women lose their jobs in the greatest numbers in the economic downturn prompted by the coronavirus crisis? Why is it always my community's local services that are cut? Why are the children in inner-city Birmingham playing on a broken swing that has been there since 2001 while in the rich London suburbs

I drive through, I see huge new climbing frames under construction in local parks?

Changing the law and, in doing so, changing the country, the continent, even the world, for the better is hard. Perhaps you have picked up this book because you think that I am the sort of politician who you can trust, and I would like to think this is true. But the truth of the matter is that, like all of us, I fuck up. I fall into tempting traps of wanting to be the most right all of the time. Fortunately, my husband is a constant voice in my ear telling me, 'Bab, don't think your shit don't stink.'

Politicians are far from perfect and we get stuff wrong. Sometimes it is wilful and because someone holds fundamentally mean views (not me you understand, I'm ever so nice), but a lot of the time we just make mistakes. And to be honest, we would probably be able to deliver a considerably better service if there wasn't such a terrible fear of making a mistake. We should be held accountable for our political decisions, without question, but for there to be an assumption of bad intention, rather than honest error, damages our ability to be brave enough to make the important changes.

The realities of political decision-making are that there are no obvious solutions and there is no such thing as a perfect law. There definitely *is* such a thing as a bad law, in my opinion – obviously not everyone would agree but, just off the top of my head: women not being able to vote; Section 28, which made it illegal for teachers to 'promote' or even acknowledge homosexual relationships as healthy family ties; laws that allow for the enslavement of people; the fact that marital rape was legal until the 1990s in the UK. These are provably bad laws. But bad laws often only become recognised as such as attitudes change; in such cases it is important that we are ready to take action to change these bad laws where possible. Of course, when making changes to a law, we can't please everyone. There is no action that can be taken where no one loses out. There is no such thing as a perfect policy and there is no such thing as an action without consequence.

Without wishing to spread the blame, while greedy politicians with bad ideas do give birth to bad laws, in many cases the politicians are doing what they perceive to be popular at the time. Many bad laws today are bad by omission as opposed to outright dangerous – the problem is usually the people who are left outside the protection of the law.

The Domestic Abuse Bill is a really good example of this. The DA Bill is a piece of legislation that seeks to do good; it wants to define all the different sorts of domestic abuse in law in a bid to tackle it. In the legislation, there are provisions to improve the number of domestic abuse refuge beds by making local councils legally bound to provide them, for example.* Bravo! What a lovely law. We could easily put this in the 'good change' column, right?

Well, no, actually we can't because this piece of legislation will not protect *all* victims of domestic violence; it does not include any provision that would ensure that a migrant victim – say a Chinese student studying microbiology at Oxford or an Australian barista – was able to access a refuge bed if her boyfriend beat the shit out of her. By omission,

---

* This was not in the original Bill; it was thanks to campaigners including me that it is in there – a case in point that it is possible to change stuff.

this piece of legislation creates a hierarchy of victims where British-born or naturalised citizens matter more. You could certainly argue – and believe me, I have – that this is therefore a discriminatory piece of legislation. So, forget what we said before about this being a good law change and let's put it in the *bad* law column, right?

There are many who would argue that I should not support this clearly discriminatory Bill on principle and do all I can to stop it passing into law until it is perfect. If I were to live and die by my principles, that's what I would do. As things are, will I vote for it? Of course I will. Not because I love discrimination – I don't. I have tried to change this law to include migrant victims for five years and so far I have failed to get the UK government to agree with me. But for now, I will vote for the things in the Bill that I do agree with and just keep on bloody well fighting for the rest. It's dissatisfying, right? I agree with you, but I wouldn't be helping anyone, including those migrant women I see week in week out, left destitute by this terrible discrimination, if I made a stand and tried to stop the Bill in its entirety. My making a stand might make me feel good, and it would get me a shit tonne of plaudits on social media. For a spell I would be a hero, but nothing would change for victims on the ground. When you make a stand in political activism, you must always make sure that it has an actual tangible outcome beyond a few retweets and the fuzzy feeling of being right.

That feeling of being right is delicious but it is not enough to save anyone. Although, by the way, on this I am bloody right, both emotionally and empirically. It is absolutely batshit that we don't offer end-to-end support to victims of domestic violence, no matter who they are. The cost of inaction is greater, in both human and financial terms, than doing something about it. A murder costs the state £4 million; a refuge bed for three months costs around £5,000; I am no mathematician, but even I can do the sums on this one. So failure to enact this policy is not just racist, it is also innumerate. I will change this law one day, and I will not mind saying 'I told you so' to the racists who didn't agree with me and left some women for dead and others actually in a grave. And you can all help. If the public showed how they agreed with me that no matter where you were born you should have a safe haven if you are being battered and raped, then the government would fold pretty fast.

To me, the above seems obvious. But I am very rarely 100 per cent certain about what is the right thing to do when I am seeking a change. Almost all of the day-to-day politics that impact your life come down to laws that are usually devised by the government: for example, whether you have a good supply of local childcare, what sort of exams you sit at what sort of school, the level of benefits available, the taxes you pay and the food that you can and cannot get. So if there is a problem in one of these areas, we have to change the law. Sometimes this is obvious – if millions of kids are going hungry in one of the richest countries in the world it seems pretty clear that we should try to do something about that – but even if the problem is clear-cut, the solution might not be. It might need a huge and unavailable logistical effort; it might mean diverting resources from elsewhere (and then – where?); it might need a bit of time to think and plan and come up with a solution that will help the most and harm the least. And even if you can come up with such a solution, you still face the battle of getting the law changed in order to implement it.

The government wins the right to change stuff by winning an election. So, if you want to change anything, big or small, the first rule is: win an election. Sounds obvious, right? Well, it has felt to me in recent years that this has been lost on my particular political party, which, up until recently, for almost all my time in Parliament, thought that winning an argument or just knowing you were right was enough. Being right changes absolutely naff all; it is having power that changes things, whether you are right or wrong. Power matters.

For lots of kindly folk who want to do good in the world, the idea of holding power can sit uncomfortably – I guess because for so many generations (and pretty much all of human history) power has often been used to do bad rather than good. But it is not the fault of power that it is and has been so cavalierly managed by those who hold it. Wanting power does not make you a megalomaniac; it's having it and acting like a dick who wants to keep it all for yourself that makes you a megalomaniac. Here, I will invoke the only guiding principle I have tried to instil in my children and the only aphorism I actually live by: don't be a dick.* I want this written on my gravestone. Having power isn't bad, it is good

* I did some sessions with Girl Guide leaders on feminist activism (read: planned to build a feminist army through a seemingly established and one-time conservative institution . . . see also the Women's Institute) where I spoke about the only mantra that matters: 'Don't Be a Dick'. They brilliantly went away and made me a 'Don't Be a Dick' badge. I was never a Girl Guide so I don't have any other badges but I am very proud of my 'Don't Be a Dick' badge. I hope to get my woodwork and global citizen badges soon.

and it is something that we should all strive to have more of. Because power births change.

So the government has power and usually – although admittedly not so much in recent years – a majority of votes in Parliament, meaning they can pretty much change anything they want and can do so with considerably more ease than any other member of Parliament who is not in government. As an ordinary citizen, if you want to see change then vote for and lobby the politicians you think will drive through that change. Get them into government.

Ordinary citizens can absolutely make governments change things. One of the ways the power-holders can be dicks is by convincing the ordinary citizen that nothing can change or that some convenient bogeyman third party (the EU, immigrants, people on benefits, the USA, China, the banks – take your pick) is the reason why they, despite being the power-holder, sadly cannot make things change. This is a lie! We, the people, can absolutely get the government to adopt things that we care about, whether these are big, broad changes or niche, specific ones.

Take state pensions, for example – these cost the state an absolute shedload. People are living much longer and drawing their pension for decades longer than they were when state pensions were first introduced in 1909.* I am here to tell you that a government who loves austerity and has cut back pretty much every welfare benefit and every single public service would absolutely love to have a tinker around with the state

---

* In 1909, when the state pension was first introduced, you only got it when you reached seventy, which in 1909 would have been a bit like winning the lottery for the average person.

pension. If they could cut it with only a bit of backlash, they absolutely would. The reason that they don't is because senior citizens, the kind of people who vote for said government, would go absolutely crackers and would probably shift who they voted for at the next election. And more than anything, the government want to stay in power. Citizens do have power over governments, even when it feels really distant. You have more power than you think. Be more pensioner!

The usual way that things change is through amendments to government Bills. A Bill is a piece of legislation that the government proposes to answer the questions of the day. This will ultimately be voted on in the House of Commons and the House of Lords, becoming an Act of Parliament if it is passed and therefore a law. Usually it is something that they have promised in the election manifesto. An example would be a pledge to increase police officers and reform the criminal justice system to be tougher on criminals and fairer to victims. That's the promise they give to the electorate. To meet that manifesto commitment, they need to turn that into a new Bill designed to deliver that commitment in law. So in this example – let's call it the Police and Crime Bill – the government would write new legislation on things like sentencing guidelines for specific crimes or enshrine in law minimum levels of policing. It might introduce new legislation about how courts will be managed or local councils provide victims' services.

The government has the power to lay whatever legislation it wants about whatever subject it wants in front of the House. Essentially it is like finding more than one way to skin a government cat. Government Bills are often quite specific about what they are trying to do. A Police and Crime Bill might be focused on giving police powers to stop protests, for example. However, as an opposition MP, I can look at this Bill and think about how I can subvert it to be about something I want to change. So I want change in the policing of domestic abuse. Domestic abuse might not be mentioned in the Bill at all, but as it is concerned with crime and policing I can now use this Bill as a potential vehicle to look at amending laws on domestic abuse.

Bills are drafted by clerks of the House of Commons and civil servants who try to avoid this very thing happening, and will be written very carefully to stop ne'er-do-well (or in fact, trying-to-do-well) MPs from employing these tactics. But this is hard to do if you want to be seen as a confident, decisive government passing big, important legislation, so in practice there is almost always a way to make a government Bill a vehicle for your action. Even though the government will try to tell you that the amendment that you want to put down is outside the scope of the Bill, MPs and Lords have become very skilled in getting around this and there is usually a way to make some noise even if you cannot legitimately amend the Bill. A large, multi-topic Bill is sometimes referred to as a 'Christmas tree Bill' – in other words, we opposition MPs try to hang loads of gaudy mismatched baubles on it in the form of opposition and cross-party amendments.

Even if the amendments or additions don't end up in the final Bill that is put before the House, the fact that you are fighting for them to be there gives you a platform to campaign on, and if you know what you are doing then the government will start to feel the pressure of your campaign.

They want their original Bill that reflects a promise they made to the electorate to pass, so they might take you up on your offer to take the bauble off *this* Christmas tree if they promise to give you another tree for it. Either that, or you manage to whack a great big piece of Poundland tinsel right across their beautiful colour-themed Liberty Christmas tree because your campaign was so strong that they had to let your amendment become part of their Bill.

These amendments are achieved through the brilliant campaigners who work with MPs, using their excellent communication strategies to win over press and public support to the point that the government just wants you to go away and stop making them look bad. MPs like me who use these tactics to change things cannot be successful without you, the brilliant general public, writing to your MPs to tell them to support our amendments or to attend our events. None of it works without the stories and testimony from the people affected; the brave people who step forward to speak up about bad things even when there is a risk to them.

This sort of campaigning for change works. Sure, it works more slowly and is a lot harder when the government have a majority, but we can still rattle the people in power into doing the right thing. Look at Marcus Rashford, whose campaign fed thousands of school children during the coronavirus crisis. Look at the women who tragically had miscarriages alone while the pandemic raged on and, through their bravery and willingness to speak up, supported by campaign groups and MPs like Cat McKinnell, managed to change the way pregnant women were being cared for during the crisis. We can change things as long as we believe that we can.

That belief needs to be backed up by a lot of legwork, however. For example, I might be looking to improve the availability of specialist support and counselling for children who are groomed and trafficked by gangs in the UK. Rather than immediately trying to amend a piece of legislation, first I would research all of the data that I need on the subject so I can prove the need for change.* I would speak to charities working to support these children, meet some of the children myself and find out where the gaps in support are. From this, I would work up a model of what needs doing to tackle this worrying rise in child trafficking in the UK. I would use this information to ask a series of public questions in the chamber of the House of Commons and I might work with back-benchers to get a debate on the subject, and for the minister concerned (in this case the Home Office minister who leads on modern slavery) to come to a public forum, address why the harm was growing faster than the support and propose action to stop it. I would then seek meetings with the relevant ministers and take along the victims and experts in the field. I would speak to journalists and broadcasters and, along with those I was campaigning with, we would tour TV studios to try to communicate to the public why this is a pressing issue.

I would hope that the noise of the campaign and the public scrutiny would appeal to the ministers early on. This does happen and I have known them to take immediate action with their budgets to address issues just like this. Lots of

---

* In 2019–20, there was a huge rise in the percentage of UK children entering the referral system as victims of human trafficking. These children have been groomed and trafficked for sex and to perform violence and drug running.

smaller changes that might not need a law change or will not cost that much are managed in this way in Parliament – private conversations and deals brokered in back rooms happen regularly. When these conversations fail and all I am getting back are warm words from the ministers about how very important this was to them, just not important enough to actually do something about, then it is only at this point that I will start to try to use the Bills and legislation going through Parliament to my advantage, and break out the Christmas decorations.

The issue of trafficked children would fall under the policy areas of human trafficking, gang violence, children's services and education. However, there may not be a Bill in front of Parliament for over a year, if not longer, that is relevant to these subject areas. It's all very well wanting to change this issue, but when all you have in front of you to work with is legislation on the UK leaving the European Union, a Bill on new welfare reforms and a Bill on how the secret services will use covert intelligence in the field, it's not that easy. So in that case, you have to comb through them to find a chink in their armour where you can crowbar in the subject you want to talk about on the floor of the chamber of the House of Commons, or in the committee scrutiny all Bills go through.

In this particular case, I would look to how the Exiting the European Union Bill talked about cross-border security and human trafficking to see if there was some way I could amend it to secure support for kids in the UK. Or I might look at how the infiltrating of organised crime gangs by police and secret services had a crossover with the world of child trafficking and find a way to amend that Bill to ensure that police forces were supported in their efforts by support in the field for victims. Like I said, it probably won't work exactly the way you want it to and you won't get the amendments you were pushing for, but ministers will often take some action if you make enough noise and they're worried that you have enough support. (Then they will take credit for it as if it was their idea all along.)

There are other ways that you can legitimately change the law from opposition, and some are more ridiculous than others. One way any backbench member of Parliament can seek to change the law from a standing start is through a Private Member's Bill. Private Member's Bills are handed out on a lottery basis. Over a couple of days at the beginning of each Parliament, an A4 hardback lined exercise book is placed in the Aye voting lobby* with the numbers 1–650 written in fancy fountain pen spaced through the book. Members of Parliament write their name next to one of the numbers, ensuring their entry in the law-changing bingo. At the time of signing, you don't have to say what law you want to change – and in fact most MPs don't know – and entry is not compulsory, but I would guess that most members of Parliament who are not in government positions of responsibility sign up. Once the deadline has passed, the clerks in Parliament pick twenty numbers out of a bag. These are the lucky MPs who will be allocated time on one of the thirteen Fridays that Parliament opens to debate so they can seek a vote on their chosen law change. (In reality, they rarely get

* The corridor you walk through during a vote in Parliament to vote yes. The corridor to vote no is simply called the No Lobby but we have not yet advanced from 'aye' to yes.

beyond the first ten as the debates tend to drag, as we'll come to below . . .)

Are you still with me? I wouldn't blame you if not because what I just wrote sounds like something out of a fantasy novel, right? *The book that changed it all . . . Many stepped up but only the chosen few honourable folk of the land were selected by fate to change the face of the laws of our sceptred isle.* If one of the thirteen sitting Fridays is Friday the thirteenth then you've got yourself the opener for a pretty good horror movie.

Winning one of the top spots in the Private Member's Ballot is not a slam dunk when it comes to changing a law: for a start, you have to win the debate to even have a vote. And if the government doesn't like your Bill, there are a number of ways that they will completely derail it, most famously by filibustering during the debate. A filibuster is a tactic that is used to prevent a vote by basically wanging on for hours so there is no time left for a vote. It's also, more understandably, called 'talking out' a Bill. The government might directly organise for one of their MPs, or sometimes even the minister, to talk out a Bill that they don't want to see becoming a law. Alternatively, they will just rely on a group of MPs who consider it a sport to spend their Friday speaking for hours on end about why parking charges in hospitals shouldn't be free for carers (to cite a real example) rather than being with their constituents.

All sides employ the filibuster tactic. I, for example, would seek to talk out a Bill that tried to ban abortion whether it was from an MP on my side or the opposition; the colour of your rosette is of no consequence in a Private Member's Bill. The way to stop the filibuster when you are trying to get your law past this first parliamentary hurdle is to make sure you have at least a hundred MPs in Parliament on your allotted Friday, which is harder than you think when MPs are not compelled to be there and most will have travelled back home to be with their constituents and their families. If you *do* make the hundred, you can interrupt a filibusterer by winning a closure motion (stay with me), which effectively leapfrogs the process and puts your proposal immediately to vote. To win the closure motion you need at least a hundred MPs voting in favour, at which point you have won the vote on whether your proposed law should go to a vote.

I can hear the voices of those of you who are still with me at this point saying 'WTF??' and I want you to know that literally nobody, not even the members of Parliament who go through this rigmarole thirteen times during a parliamentary session, think this system is any good. Nobody offers you any training on this when you are elected and to this day I find it absolutely baffling. But luckily there is a breed of MP who knows every tiny little thing about parliamentary procedure and what the hell is going on. I tried to learn all this stuff, I tried to keep across it – but I have no hope. As my mother's generation of feminists used to say, 'Life is too short to peel a mushroom.'* So too is my political life too short to try to understand why the bloody hell we do some things the way we do and why we don't change the stuff that is clearly ridiculous. Some battles I just don't have the energy to fight. So while thousands of people are still being raped and receiving

---

* Why would anyone peel a mushroom? I cannot believe for a second that people used to or perhaps still do this.

no justice, for example, I am going to focus on that; perhaps one day I will get around to a) trying to understand arcane parliamentary rules and b) scrapping them.

Having lost my rag slightly, it is worth saying that some pretty important laws have been changed using this mechanism. In 1965, it was a Private Member's Bill that brought about an end to the death penalty, and in 1967 this was the way that abortion was legalised. Private members of Parliament are often considerably braver than the governments of the day, who worry about polling and public backlash considerably more, and so they can go out on a limb and simply get things done.

On the day we were queuing up to sign the Private Member's Bill ballot book in 2019, I bumped into the prime minister of our country, one Mr Boris Johnson, in the lobby. He, of course, has greater opportunity than others to change the law but at the time was finding it tricky to get anything through the Commons thanks to having no overall majority, a situation he had inherited from Theresa May's disastrous 2017 general election. He had recently been defeated on a number of votes and was looking decidedly neutered.

Even a man as casual (scruffy mess) as Boris Johnson is afforded a certain reverence by colleagues on his own side once he holds the position of prime minister. People who, just weeks before, you would have had a laugh and a joke with in the corridors of the palace become almost god-like when they are adorned with power. When a prime minister walks the halls of Westminster people move deferentially out of the way, like a silent order of nuns as the pope approaches. It must be pretty lonely, because people literally start looking at the floor as you approach and refer to you as 'Prime Minister' rather than by your name. I would hate it – and for this reason I don't act like this. Plus, reverence is not my strong suit.

On this day, as I went to sign the legislative book of fate, I said to the prime minister, 'I know you're struggling to pass any laws but has it really come to this? You have to try and get heard through the Private Member's Ballot?' To be fair to him, he took it as the gentle ribbing it was intended to be, while his flunkies looked horrified at my insolence. He went on to ask what he would have to offer me before I would back his Brexit plans and we chatted agreeably while not agreeing at all for about ten minutes. Meanwhile, the silent nuns hung about, probably wondering if they needed to take the piss a bit more in order to get an audience with the prime minister where he ends up essentially begging for their support. In that situation I had the power – because of the hung Parliament, the prime minister needed me considerably more than I needed him. Although to be fair, I would be cheeky regardless of where the balance of power lay.

I segue for the sake of an anecdote perhaps but actually my encounter with the prime minister (of which I have had many, with varying outcomes) is an important part of how things change. We have to try to get on with each other in politics for the sake of actually getting stuff done. This is rarely talked about, as the brittleness and vitriol of politics form the bulk of the desired spectator sport. Of course, I loathe and detest a lot of what my opponents (and some of those on my own side) think and do. Just like you probably hate some of your work colleagues. But if I refused to work with the Tories on anything then I would only be doing a service to my ego, which frankly does not need any more servicing. I would be failing the people who need me to go to Parliament and change things.

The prime minister has more power than me, therefore I need to convince him to give me what I want. I need Conservative back benchers to support my causes because the prime minister is far more worried about the dissent of his own side than me shouting at him. Also, some of them are good people and are right about things and our difference of opinion is due to our different upbringings. I know for example that if I go publicly hard and heavy on the rhetoric with the Justice Minister Alex Chalk, I will force him into having to take a position against me, even if he agrees with me; however, if I just pick up the phone and have a chat with him, we can usually get to a place where we are both happy and can move forward. This happens with one minister or another pretty much weekly. Yes, sometimes I have to take to Twitter to directly shame ministers for leaving hundreds of poor kids in deprived areas off school without computer equipment to do lessons at home,* but often a good and healthy working relationship with the ministers is a faster and more efficient solution. Alas, I will never have this with the Education Secretary Gavin Williamson because he is an arse who only cares about himself and how he can move up the ladder. Oh, the things he could achieve if only he cared about the progression of our country's children with the same fervour. He doesn't.

---

* That shaming had hundreds of computers delivered to my constituency within four hours when the schools had previously been told it wasn't possible. Turns out public shaming makes things possible pretty sharpish.

The law changes remarkably slowly. To a member of the public this does not necessarily seem like the case. You can wake up one morning to a completely new set of rules about seatbelts in your cars, or if you can go to the shops on a Sunday, or the pub after 11 p.m., and it seems as if the law changed overnight. The reality is that this will have been preceded by at least a decade of the policy idea forming, at least five years of the policy idea getting an airing in Parliament to prepare members and, depending on the policy, about three years of parliamentary debate, committees and scrutiny.

The only time I had really been cognisant of how long a law-change takes before I became one of the people who sat through endless committees and pre-legislative scrutiny and was happily just a citizen who had stuff done to me was regarding the smoking ban in pubs and restaurants. In 2004, I was working in a pub where we chatted politics across the bar, no doubt, but the biggest political thing that would happen each year was the announcing of the budget, when we would find out if beer and fags had gone up in price. Beyond this, we didn't particularly feel engaged in the process of law.

One morning shift, as we stocked up ready for opening and walked around placing ashtrays on the tables, my manager sat at the end of the bar going through the post. She opened up a consultation document from either the government or the brewery asking us about the possibility of a new law that would ban smoking in public places, including pubs. She started taking soundings from the staff as she filled out the form. It was a fairly official-looking document and I have to say I'm not sure how seriously we took it, but we all piped up with our opinions. As someone who smoked at least twenty fags a day at the time and wanted to be able to do that in the middle of a shift, I gave my response to the proposal in no uncertain terms. If memory serves, I think I am right in saying that all of us who worked in the pub at the time were smokers, so it's possible we were a slightly biased crowd.

As the day drew on, we asked the punters what they thought and a similar pattern of disdain for the idea played out. This was not scientifically done and we almost certainly couched the question as: 'Can you believe the government wants us to stop smoking in the pub?' We probably directed our straw poll at every punter with a fag in their mouth. I am sure that my boss filled in the paperwork with more reasoned arguments, such as how it would affect our ability to trade, as it was a small pub with approximately one square metre of outside space that already housed a bin. But safe to say, whatever the arguments, we did not care for the smoking ban.[*]

I remember how appalled we were by this suggested impingement on our liberty. It felt like a spectre of doom on the immediate horizon that was going to imminently put our jobs at risk and see us huddled in the cold at the bus stop outside the pub. In fact, what happened was that three years passed by and the smoking ban was not introduced until July 2007. By this time, I had largely packed in smoking, had given birth to my first child, was about to have my second

---

[*] I was wrong. The smoking ban is an excellent idea and I fully support it now. Never trust a politician who will not admit how wrong they were about something. I was always stunned by the way in which Jeremy Corbyn was praised for always thinking the same way throughout his career and sticking to his 'principles', as if not changing your mind about changing situations was somehow a good thing. It isn't. I still smoke the occasional fag and am more than happy to do it outside so as not to harm others. My twenty-year-old self would have disagreed.

and, as the mother of a toddler, hadn't seen the inside of a pub for many a year. I was now all for the idea of my child not breathing in people's cigarette smoke when I went out to a café and was more worried about finding the childcare that would allow me to do a shift of work anywhere than I was about being able to have a fag break on a shift.

What can seem like a sudden and ill-thought-out change in the law is usually something that has been discussed in both Houses of Parliament for many years. Although there can be good reason for this (certain decisions should not be rushed – we will come on to this), this glacial rate of change is without question the most maddening thing about my job. I am not a woman who possesses even one iota of natural patience. I have had to train myself not to expect things to happen quickly in politics, otherwise I would have packed it all in and gone back to working behind a bar. Although to be fair, this is also a place where other people's impatience used to really grind my gears – yes, I can see you waving that tenner* at me, but as you can see, I am serving someone else who was here first!

I remember once talking to Harriet Harman, who has spent her life trying to use the House of Commons to improve the lives of women. She was elected when I was one year old, as one of only twenty female MPs, and is still in the Commons today. In this particular conversation, I

---

* When I worked in a pub a tenner would have easily bought you four pints of lager; now you'd be lucky to get two. This is a good example of how politics affects all of our lives: to anyone who thinks taxes, duties, inflation, trade and the economy don't really have anything to do with them, they are literally everywhere and in everything.

was losing my rag about how the government still had not implemented mandatory reporting on the gender pay gap, despite promising action for seven years. I asked her how she remained so calm and patient. She said, 'Jess, it took me eight years to win the argument for the hairdressers in Parliament to offer haircuts to women, and when we won that battle it felt like a real victory that we had managed to force through. I have just got used to waiting.' This, dear reader, is why Harriet Harman has lasted thirty-nine years as a member of Parliament, at the time of writing, and why I will likely last much less time, unless I learn not to let all the bloody maddening delay, obfuscation and stupid road blocks stress me out so much. It is simply not good for my health to be as annoyed as I am on a near-daily basis.

During one of the many votes on Brexit, I found myself speaking to the veteran Labour MP Sir George Howarth in the tearoom at 11 p.m. I asked him, 'How did you used to do this all the time when Parliament used to sit all night? I'd be dead if I had to do this all night, every night, all week.' The MP peered at me over the top of his paper, took a sip of his tea and replied in his delightfully droll Merseyside tone, 'Well, yes, you might have been dead. Many more MPs used to die back then.'* It does sometimes feel as if the slowness and the madness of the place is going to kill me, but I had hoped it would be more metaphorical than actual. I like being a politician but I'm not sure I like it *that* much.

Having established that nothing happens fast in Parliament,

---

* Even today, it is harder to get life insurance as a member of Parliament than it is for many other professions. This also extends to securing a mortgage and, weirdly, car insurance. Maybe we are just all really bad drivers.

the exception is of course if there is a sudden global pandemic, in which case fundamental laws can be overturned quicker than you can say 'personal protective equipment'. It's remarkable, really, how quickly we can change laws when it is needed. This is an argument you will be hearing me put to ministers for at least the next ten years, beginning as we enter the third year of committees and meetings on the Domestic Abuse Bill and are still being told that we simply have to wait to make the legislation work. Hundreds of women will have been murdered in their homes while that piece of legislation drags its way into its fourth year of discussion.

Progress is being made in the Domestic Abuse Bill, albeit slowly. A new clause was recently added by an amendment I laid on behalf of the brilliant campaigners and cross-party group of MPs who took up the case of a young woman called Natalie Connelly. Her partner left her for dead in his home after inflicting heinous violence against her. His defence for leaving her overnight to die at the bottom of his stairs while he slept upstairs was that she had consented to it as part of a sex game. In Natalie's honour, campaigners are seeking to change the law by inserting a new clause that would disallow the accused from seeking to enter a defense that the victim died in an incidence of 'rough sex' which she had consented to. This law has so far taken longer to progress through Parliament than the time her killer served in jail: he served twenty-two months for her killing and is already out of prison. At the time of writing (and let's face it, probably at hardback and paperback publication), the law that would stop this man claiming that Natalie asked to be murdered remains unchanged; while the clause has been added, the Bill is yet to be passed, and remains stuck in some committee somewhere in a room where ancient gargoyles look down on it.

So why does it all take so long? Well, there are a number of good reasons behind this. The first is that laws made in a rush are not necessarily a good thing. There is a huge amount of logistics that might need to be implemented to support a change and many complications that need to be ironed out to make sure that a policy idea will actually work. You can't make new immigration laws, for example, without employing many more immigration officers to implement them. You can't make new licensing hours laws without ensuring that there will be enough police to patrol the streets at the new pub closing times. When you change the law you have to ensure that you have considered all of the consequences for *other* laws that exist – such as employment laws prescribing the hours people can work – and how you are going to pay for it, not just this year but for many years into the future.

Not all laws last forever and we tinker with them all the time. Some even have specific sunset clauses in them so that they will only last for a certain period of time – such as while the country is hosting a big sports event or, in the case of some equalities laws, until such a time as we would hope to have achieved equality in that area (hahaha).* However, most laws

---

* There is a sunset clause in the Equality Act 2010 that stopped the use of positive discrimination, such as all-women's shortlists by political parties, by 2015, because I guess when it was drafted there was an expectation that women would by that point have political equality. I am writing this in 2021 and we still don't: only 220 out of 650 MPs are women. In 2015, the sunset clause was extended to 2030, so hope springs eternal. Maybe by then we will have 250, but I wouldn't bet on it.

are made with a view that they will last at least a couple of decades, so a fair amount of scrutiny is needed to make sure you are not imposing legislation on the future that you cannot guarantee will be workable.

This all seems reasonable. Less understandable are the maddening, inevitable and repetitive battles. Members of Parliament are a strange breed who, like horses, must not be startled by sudden changes. This is especially true of those who went into Parliament with the specific desire to conserve things the way they are (the clue is in the party name). Like children, many MPs need to be drip-fed an idea for a very long time before they are willing to countenance even having a conversation about a law being changed. A bit like the stages of grief, there are some definable stages that many politicians must go through before entering into such a conversation. These are:

The nanny state stage: No matter what it is you might seek to change, there are politicians, ably assisted by their reliable media outriders, ready to deride any change as the actions of the nanny state. Let us just pause for a moment to consider this phrase, which has become common parlance in political discourse. It probably makes perfect sense if you live in a turn-of-the-century novel and have a well-meaning but firm governess telling you what to do all the time, but 99 per cent of the population have never had a nanny – not this sort, anyway. Where I live, 'nanny' is your mum's mum, not a woman who lives in your home to provide firm but rosy-cheeked spoon-feeding childcare. The fact that this term has become the shorthand rolled out whenever the state tries to intervene speaks volumes about the way in which politics is still ruled by the upper classes.

In this stage, you will be met with a chorus of politicians telling you that suggesting, for example, that employers should be bound by law to prevent sexual harassment in their workplaces* is the nanny state seeking to control everything. It isn't. I am not telling you what to wear, who to love,† what you should eat for your dinner, who you should be or what music you should like. I am saying that you shouldn't turn a blind eye when one of your executives gropes a woman in the post room. Look at me trying to spoon-feed the public.

The 'whataboutery' stage: After everyone has accused you of being an oppressive Mary Poppins, you will encounter the second stage, at which you are asked to consider the unintended consequences of your suggested law change, the 'what about's. These will range from the sublime to the ridiculous. The sublime is the detailed and thoughtful consideration of a reasonable unintended consequence. A good example of this would be that if you pass a law that obliges all local councils to provide refuge accommodation, you may find that some councils will source the money to provide this by defunding other community-based services for victims of domestic abuse. This is worth worrying about (and is in fact

---

* This is a law I have been attempting to change for three years, so it is a mere sapling in the forest of legislative change. If your employer does nothing to prevent you being sexually harassed or worse at work, then it's fine, they are currently not doing anything illegal; if they don't prevent you being harmed by hot liquid, however, that *would* be illegal. Cups of tea are more dangerous than predatory bosses, apparently. We are all just waiting for the #teatoo movement.
† Incidentally, the exact same politicians who wang on about the nanny state did for a long time think that people should be told who they could and couldn't marry and are often the very individuals who voted against same-sex couples being able to get hitched. They like nanny a lot when she agrees with them.

something I am very worried about and have sought to amend any legislation to ensure that *both* have to be provided) and is an example of good scrutiny.

Then there are the ridiculous unintended consequences that might be thrown back at you in debate. For example, an MP saying that allowing gay marriage could lead to the unintended consequence of undermining heterosexual marriage. This was in fact said by a lot of people, who are presumably not that confident in their own heterosexual marriages. I was married to a man before gay marriage; I am still married to him now; I have noticed no discernible difference in my marriage. The most crackers unintended consequence of gay marriage put forward by a parliamentarian came from Lord Tebbit, who said it would lead to the possibility of a lesbian queen giving birth to a future monarch by artificial insemination. For a start, so what? And second, how do we know that hasn't already happened? We don't watch live inseminations of the heir to the throne and, frankly, how anyone is conceived is none of my business. Lord Tebbit doubled down with the weird assertion that the legislation could also allow him to marry his son to escape inheritance tax. Er, no, it couldn't, mate. (Although interesting that inheritance-tax dodging was his go-to when thinking about two people getting married.) Not to mention the number of heterosexual couples over the years who have used their marriage to dodge taxes and consequences. Philip Green's entire fortune is in his wife's name after some creative tax-efficiency schemes.

In most cases, the politicians who just plain don't agree with what you are proposing won't even bother to come up with what the unintended consequences could be. They just pose the question as if you are an idiot who hasn't spent years researching, thinking and testing your idea. They will say, 'Ah, the honourable lady has not considered the unintended consequences . . .' and just leave it hanging in the air as if it is checkmate. Ministers will patronise you by saying things like, 'It is all well and good that the honourable lady is passionate about this subject, indeed we all are [they aren't], however, in government we must first and foremost look at all the unintended consequences of such a change.' Which is of course true – but unfortunately they are going to do sod all about actually looking into them. They should just say, 'We are not going to do this because we don't want to.' I'd prefer that. Instead, they have to make out the reason they won't make a perfectly reasonable change is because they are cleverer than you, rather than because they are meaner that you.

The review stage: By this point, you have fought your corner, batting off all the idiots saying that fighting for women's rights will lead to donkeys being able to become primary school teachers, and you've weeded out all of those saying this is just the nanny state trying to control us all with a crazy oppressive regime. The public have swung behind you, a normally conservative newspaper has backed your campaign and the government has decided that it cannot bear listening to you wanging on righteously anymore and it is going to show you a bit of leg. That is when you get offered a review.

An email will be sent from the relevant minister informing you that the government is going to launch a consultation and review into, say, sexual harassment in the workplace, or migrant victims of domestic abuse destitution, or paternity leave for new fathers. These are all issues I have raised in the past, by the way, none of which have yet seen any change in law. The review into sexual harassment in the workplace following the global #MeToo movement has been now overseen by three different Secretaries of State for Women and Equalities and not a single law has changed that would make it any less easy to grope someone, sack them for speaking up and then silence them with a non-disclosure agreement, meaning they can never speak of it again. But don't worry about those wandering hands at work – there is a review going on, which I am sure makes everyone feel much safer.

The process is usually that a government department will put out a survey to the general public for consultation. They will then allow a series of civil servants and relevant government ministers to write a report into what was found and what they propose to do about it. Some reviews draft in external experts and independent parties to head it up or a board of experts is brought in to oversee it. For example, the Lammy Review, chaired by David Lammy MP, is an independent review of the treatment of, and outcomes for, Black, Asian and minority ethnic (BAME) individuals in the criminal justice system. Most reviews that are wholly led by government departments will simply proscribe a problem rather than suggest any firm solutions. Independent reviews are usually better as they tend to be more robust in recommendations and critique, and conclude with a very detailed set of recommendations of necessary law changes and adjustments to legislation. Reviews usually take around three to six months and have a period of six weeks of consultation with the public, usually through an online survey.

A review is a necessary thing to do if you are going to

change the law and a consultation of the public who would be affected and experts in the field is absolutely the right thing to do. However, the reality is that in lots of cases, the offer of a review is the place where change goes to die. At least half of the reviews I have seen the government launch were simply a way of trying to make the issue go away with the illusion of action. There will not have been a single expert who gave evidence to the review on migrant victims of domestic abuse who would agree with the government's position that the victims should essentially be ignored. And yet no action has been taken. So why even bother asking for people's opinions on the matter? Pity the poor civil servant who spends months working on a review that they know the government will just pop on a shelf and hope that everyone forgets about it.

Parliament is full of cul-de-sacs and weird processes that pop up like a banana skin on the road, waiting to trip you up as you try to enact change. It is maddening that a group of people who got involved in politics because they wanted to change the world become so bound and tied by rules, process and the pervading wind of popular opinion that they can be rendered completely impotent. The ability of Parliament and individual MPs to change things will always play second fiddle to the government of the day, who have the power to change so much for the better but rarely, in my time in politics, at least, use it. I must be fair here: I quite like that you have to reuse your plastic bags these days, but then my constituents can afford less shopping than they used to, so they need fewer bags anyway.

Imagine having the power to actually change anything you wanted. You could come up with a solution for social care, or support for the elderly and disabled. You could make sure people were treated fairly at work or could definitely access care and support if they had been abused or harmed. Imagine having that power and not using it. My position means that I get a platform to shout about this stuff, but we all have the power to change laws, to fight for better, to demand more at work, in our towns, cities and across our country. We all have the power to make our politicians really work for us. The greatest trick ever played by the powerful was to convince the population that we couldn't change things, when the truth is that we can.

6

Being Diplomatic: MPs Abroad

'MPs given hundreds of overseas trips worth more than £2,000,000 in two years', screams the *Metro*. 'MPs sign up for £2m of free overseas trips – You can see how many trips your MP has accepted in the year since the election by searching below', points out the BBC, complete with a handy tool to look up where your MP is going and who is paying for it – the taxpayer, a company or a foreign state.* 'How MPs' foreign junkets have cost taxpayers £1.4m', exclaims the *Daily Mail*, who is less concerned about rogues paying for MPs' holidays and more worried about the taxpayer funding it. Now, I can see why people wouldn't want us wasting money on foreign jaunts, but are we seriously suggesting that MPs should not travel as part of their work? It is a global job.

Don't get me wrong, I realise that foreign travel is a major perk of my job; one of the best things about being a member of Parliament is the fact that we get to see the world. Not the holiday resorts or tourist spots, of course, we get to see a

---

* I put my own name in and it came up with one trip to Israel and the Palestinian territories I had been on, which was paid for and organised by a charity supporting medical aid for Palestinians. I have never been on a trip paid for by a business or a foreign state.

foreign country as it really is. Were my husband and I to go to Paris, we would in all likelihood be stuck on the tourist trails, shuffling along in line to see the *Mona Lisa* and paying over the odds for a bang average piece of pizza not far from the Eiffel Tower. *C'est la vie*. All of the travel I have done as a member of Parliament, however, has been the exact opposite; it has almost exclusively taken me to the kind of places a tourist would not normally go.

Most parliamentary trips abroad are organised by All Party Parliamentary Groups, international development charities seeking to highlight a particular issue abroad, such as female genital mutilation or the refugee crisis (like I said: not a tourist trip), or by select committees undertaking enquiries into how other countries do things. There are also two organisations that operate out of Parliament who work to foster relations and learning across borders: these are the Commonwealth Parliamentary Association Group (CPAG), which focuses on the Commonwealth countries, and the Inter-Parliamentary Union (IPU), which is global.

Every week or so, CPAG and IPU advertise delegations to foreign countries and MPs can apply for a place, expressing their particular reason for wanting to go. So, for example, if you have a big Chinese company in your constituency, providing jobs and investment, you might want to travel to Shanghai on a planned delegation in order to build further ties. This is reciprocal and most of my work with CPAG and IPU actually takes place in the UK, where we hold sessions for visiting members of Parliament from around the world: we've hosted delegations of Pakistani women's caucuses, newly elected Lebanese women interested in equality, representatives of Lesotho who want to talk about how we scrutinise governments on public accounts. It's essentially a massive information-sharing shindig where representatives from around the world can learn from each other.

Most travel by MPs is all completely legit and is genuinely for the betterment of relations and industry across international borders, or to find out about what British aid is funding and what more is needed, or to look at a particularly good model that is working well elsewhere – housing policy in Germany, for example, or the eradication of a specific disease in Angola. It is all part of research into governance, into furthering our international relationships, learning from other countries and vice versa. And believe me when I say that it is not a holiday, but instead usually fourteen-hour days where you eat a lot of sweaty sandwiches on a minibus travelling through the desert with another MP you do not like who keeps on using inappropriate language to refer to the locals and tries to pull rank on you in discussions. (You might be older and posher and more male than me, but you are no more senior as an MP than I am and I do not have to follow your frankly ludicrous lead when we meet the ambassador.) Generally speaking, these are not the gang of people I would choose to go away with. Although, having said that, on many occasions I have gotten to know and really like some of the people I have travelled with for work.

There is of course another sort of trip that MPs take – the less legitimate sort. I cannot write about these with any inside knowledge as I have never been on one. These trips are something of a lottery: if you take a five-star trip off a rich mate who is in bed with a dodgy regime, you will probably get in trouble – or you might become the prime minister; I guess it depends on your luck and breeding. Alas, no one has offered me and my family a month-long, all-expenses-paid holiday to Sri Lanka and no foreign officials have ever approached me for an off-the-record meeting when I just happened to be on a family holiday in Israel. I must be putting out the wrong vibes; I like to call it morality.

I have, however, been on some amazing trips to parts of the world, where I have had the opportunity to see things I could never have imagined I would be allowed access to. In Kenya, I didn't just get to go on safari and see the sights and sounds of Nairobi, I was able to access the lives of prostituted women in rural communities and listen to stories that reach far beyond glossy brochures. In Palestine, I did not simply visit the Banksy hotel in East Jerusalem, but got to break bread with the activists who are seeking justice for an occupied people. When I visit countries as an MP, I'm invited to meet with dignitaries and people with power; I go beyond the rope in the palaces and legislative buildings that are open to a touring public.

The trips tend to follow a similar pattern no matter where you are going in the world. Whether you are travelling as part of a parliamentary delegation or with a development charity, the first thing that you notice is that outside of Europe they take visiting dignitaries pretty seriously. At Heathrow airport you will have been treated exactly the same as everyone else as you wait to board the plane to Tanzania or Beijing – just another face in the crowd, no special treatment. You will have met your fellow delegates at the KFC or Giraffe restaurant, where you were given your itineraries while drinking bad coffee and checking your passport for the millionth time, before taking your seat in economy class. I have only once flown business class on a parliamentary trip (or, in fact, on any trip in my life) and that was because we were flying through the night and were due at a meeting as soon as we landed. As far as the UK end of our trip is concerned, we are just ordinary travellers, nothing particularly fancy about it. When we arrive at our destination, though, it's a different story. In every country outside Europe I have ever travelled to on a parliamentary trip, I have been treated like some sort of international superstar once we landed.

What I did not know before I was an MP was that most airports have a hidden layer: palatial, marble-floored, leather-throne furnished rooms where groups of dignitaries and, if the décor is anything to go by, West Coast rappers and their entourage are taken once they land. You sit in luxury in these rooms as waiting staff come and offer you fresh coffee and local delicacies, while someone from the local government office or the British consulate in that country does all of the customs and order checks for you. Then someone fetches your bags and loads them onto the air-conditioned minibus ready to take you from the secret dignitary exit, thereby sidestepping all of the ordinary lugging your suitcase through miles of airport corridors and competing with your many fellow travellers for the single taxi waiting outside. Travelling as an MP is the single most bougie thing I have ever done and I can see how this could turn anyone into a massive diva.*

* There is always one person on every trip who is really precious and makes all sorts of demands on the staff about the noise in their room or the quality of the food. I have only ever been on one trip where no one was being a massive baby; when I went to China everyone was really lovely, to the point where I looked around and thought, *No one is being the twat on this trip.* Then I worried that perhaps it was me. There is always one.

Incidentally, when dignitaries below the rank of prime minister or president visit the UK, which is a pretty frequent occurrence, they aren't welcomed into a luxurious VIP lounge at the airport – we don't so much as arrange them a taxi from Gatwick. This will either make us seem down to earth and of the people or massive meanies.

In pretty much every country that you visit, when you first arrive you will be invited to an event at the residence of the British ambassador, the top Foreign Office official in that country. This could be anything from breakfast, lunch or dinner to a fancy drinks party. Imagine an event and a venue reminiscent of the 1930s or '40s and you will have some idea of what these things are like. They are exactly like the Ferrero Rocher adverts, although to my great disappointment I have never been offered a Ferrero Rocher by an ambassador and had the opportunity to say the famous line. There is still time for me to be really spoiled.

The residencies of these diplomats are usually palatial mansions behind high gates on roads where other diplomats live. Colonial-style buildings like miniature White Houses, often with large, manicured gardens. Inside, the tables are laid with pure white linen, set with pure white British porcelain, and gold cutlery glints next to sparkling crystal glassware. Your seat will be marked by a place card embossed with the UK government crest in gold and a picture of the Queen will invariably hang on a wall. It's a throwback to the idea of what it was to be British a century ago; while Britain has moved on, our outposts remain perfectly preserved and frozen in time, representing Britain as it was when there was such a thing as the British Empire, instead of how it is now.

No matter whether it is breakfast, lunch or dinner, you are eating with the ambassador and so you will always be served multiple courses that are quintessentially British, although sometimes with a local twist. This was my experience in Kenya, Tanzania and Beijing; the only slightly more relaxed welcome I have had was in Jerusalem. We arrived there quite late in the evening, so it was a more informal drinks event. I was hot after the sweltering walk to the ambassador's residence and dehydrated from the plane, so I drank way too much gin and tonic, far too quickly. This building didn't seem to have any of the hallmarks of other ambassadorial residences; it was more '70s movie set than British country estate, all low brown leather sofas that are hard to get out of, especially when you have drunk too much and eaten too little (the salted almonds, delicious as they were, were no match for the G&T).

These meetings are not purely pantomime, they are an opportunity to start your delegation with a frank conversation with the local British officials. They will inform you about the situation in that country and brief you on your upcoming meetings: what some of the people you will meet from the local government might say; what you should be looking out for and what would be helpful to ascertain. The ambassador will often have arranged for other local officials to come along and meet you – for example, academics in the field of conflict in the Middle East or the head of the local aid agencies managing a local refugee crisis – so that you can arm yourself with facts and knowledge relevant to the rest of your trip. For example, in Beijing we were briefed on questions we would be asked regarding the fact that British boats had, seemingly, entered Chinese waters at the time. They are essentially very high-level briefing meetings with fancy china and calligraphy name plates.

My favourite ambassador's residence that I ever visited is in New York and is the home of the British Ambassador to the United Nations (and his family). It is an amazing New York apartment with beautiful pieces of British modern art on the walls. The buildings are always grand and have a slightly formal air from the government business conducted there, but you can often catch glimpses, through a window into the grounds or a door left ajar, of the family that lives there: an abandoned scooter in the yard or a stack of Disney DVDs among the first editions of great British literature. I remember when I was a kid, sitting on the stairs staring through the bannisters when my parents had friends over for drinks in the evening – it always seemed so glamorous. Imagine growing up in the ambassador's residence, where your parents' guests are the presidents and prime ministers of nations.

At a drinks and nibbles reception in the ambassador's home in New York, I met Ban Ki-moon, the Secretary General of the United Nations at the time. It was during the UN Congress on the Commission for the Status of Women and I was there to support British efforts to agree global goals and standards on things like child marriage, women's reproductive rights and women's economic disadvantage. Ban Ki-moon and I chatted briefly about global gender equality and I cheekily asked him which nation was the most difficult to get onside on these matters. I told him I wouldn't tell and that he was free to offload his annoyances on me and tell me who was pissing him off. Ever the diplomat, he giggled at my insolence and said he couldn't possibly say but there was considerably more than one nation that was tricky.

I think a lot of people where I work may read this and be aghast (once again) at my perceived lack of reverence for an individual or institution that I am supposed to bow my head to. But I am not naturally a formal politician and I think we need all sorts in politics. Personally, I find that using informality, humour and being upfront and a bit cheeky with people, regardless of their status in some old-world hierarchy, works; it helps people trust, or at least understand, me. It is not failsafe of course, and some people are deeply affronted by me, but sometimes I think the ice needs to be broken in these very formal settings so that people can speak more freely. So I'll crack a joke.

One of my most memorable foreign trips was to China. Prior to travel, we will be briefed by members of the Foreign Office team in the UK on what to expect, what sort of security we will need and how we should behave in certain situations. The briefing for China is, essentially, expect to be spied on – so don't take your phone with you and don't accept gifts, as they could have bugs in them. There is also the possibility of being framed in certain countries through proffered drugs or honey traps, where prostituted women are sent to your room,* giving the host country intel that they could use to blackmail you in the future. I heard tell of this

---

* Remember all those stories about Trump and prostitutes peeing on beds in Russia? That's the kind of thing we're talking about. Nations will instigate salacious intel on persons of interest in order to have leverage and power in the future. It's a real thing, even if it seems more like something out of *House of Cards*.

exact thing happening in China, when a female prostitute was sent to knock on the hotel door of a visiting British MP and was turned away repeatedly. I actually found this story quite comforting; it made me considerably less scared of the intelligence China is holding on us, as the MP in question was an openly gay man who I am sure would not have slept with any prostitute but was certainly not going to be entrapped by an attractive woman. Maybe she had the wrong room.*

Before going to Beijing, I was prepared for many situations: I was told of the formalities and risks and what I should and shouldn't do and say. It was heavier than most briefings MPs receive when visiting a country with whom we are at peace. As usual, on arrival in China, we visited the ambassador for further briefings and warnings, and to eat lovely food and drink English breakfast tea, before heading off to the Great Hall of the People in Tiananmen Square. Although built in the 1950s, the Great Hall has the aura of a building that has always been there and it makes Buckingham Palace look positively homely. Once you are inside, it is just a series of huge corridors and massive hall spaces that are all eerily empty, awaiting being set up for particular use. As we made our way

---

* It is worth pointing out that in this case the MP was entirely innocent. However, I have heard tell of MPs on delegations sleeping with local prostitutes. The funny thing about sexually exploiting people outside of your own country is that people seem to think it lets them off the hook for their behaviour – a bit like how spending foreign currency often doesn't seem like real money, or calories you eat on holiday don't count. Apparently, people can nattily convince themselves that poor foreign women are not like normal women and exploiting their poverty while away from home is absolutely fine. Following a number of parliamentarians coming forward to the sexual harassment enquiry with tales of fellow MPs on delegations sampling the local women, we had to have it explicitly written into the code of conduct for MPs that this is forbidden.

through the ground floor, each hall that we passed through had one wall dominated by a huge mural or tapestry, each depicting different regional landscapes in China: dramatic paintings of rockfaces with the Great Wall of China picked out in detail, or huge forest scenes that scream how vast a country this is. Big and powerful is the message you get from the building.

Every room in the Great Hall of the People is very ornate and the building itself is breathtaking, but its name seemed ambitious at best, as it was completely empty as I walked through, other than for the women who walk silently along the corridors to pour the tea in various meetings. It was quiet and controlled, far more so than any other political congress building I have been in. There was no security to get through on entry: we just pulled up at the doors in our cars and sauntered straight up the steps. There were no people milling around, as you might expect even in the ceremonial buildings of a legislature. In Parliament there are always hundreds of people strolling around; the US Congress is the same and likewise every European Parliament building I have visited. Not here. In Beijing, there were just vast spaces, calm and quiet. I guess that is what total state control gets you.

Our initial visit to the Great Hall of the Not Many People was to meet with dignitaries from the Chinese Communist Party. We were walked through a vast hallway to one of the huge halls where a horseshoe of lounge chairs had been set up. We each had our own side table for our obligatory tea, which was served to us in unison like a ballet. Imagine social distancing meets a really high-end old people's home, where comfy armchairs are arranged discreetly apart but so that everyone is facing each other and can have a nice chat. That cosy chat would range from the relations between our countries, the Chinese government's investments across Asia and Africa, both our nations' roles in the efforts to curb climate change, the cultural exchange between the UK and China through reciprocal foreign student programmes, the autonomy of Taiwan and Hong Kong and the sticky issue of Chinese human rights abuses, specifically in Henan province concerning the labour camps holding the Turkic Muslim Uyghurs population.*

As we filed in, four male and two female British MPs, we took our seats on our side of the horseshoe. It was immediately clear that there would be no female representation in the Chinese delegation. Six fellas in nearly identical suits (tbf all suits look the same to me) sat in their comfy seats, though only one of them actually spoke; the others simply listened. I asked a question about the lack of women at the top of the Communist Party and what that meant for the women in China, as well as in the countries where China sought to invest in road, rail and infrastructure. I wanted to know how they ruled for women in our world. I don't speak much Mandarin – bar 'hello', 'goodbye', 'thank you' and a couple

* On the issue of the Uyghur population, we were told repeatedly in a number of meetings that the camps in Xinjiang were not forced labour but vocational education facilities. I asked if I could return to visit them sometime, to see if they would be suitable for the British to promote these educational facilities at home for foreign student enrolment. This was a reasonable request. Many of the conversations we had with Chinese officials were about the number of Chinese students studying in the UK and how they would like to see that reciprocated with British students coming into China. I also followed up with the fact that I was keen for my own sons to have an international education and so I was very interested to see these facilities. I was told that they were sure it could be arranged. It wasn't. It never will be.

of swear words my mate who lived in China taught me – so I asked this question through our very delightful young female translator, who I am certain made it much more polite in tone than I had managed in English. I was told that Chairman Mao believed that women held up half the sky and that gender equality was not an issue here in China. I was told that women's representation in the Communist Party was good, just perhaps not in this meeting.* They did at least have the good grace to laugh awkwardly.

This was the first day of our trip in Beijing, and thereafter, I never once attended another meeting where there was not a woman present, be it with foreign officials, education departments or international aid agencies. Not a woman who spoke, you understand, but one or two who had clearly been drafted in to attend so that I would never ask the question again. Face-saving and being seen to respond, I was told, is of vital importance in Chinese culture. The women looked largely bored of the meetings and I felt I had done them a terrible disservice in demanding their presence and that there was now a group of civil servant women who would have to silently attend all meetings thanks to this bloody British woman.

I could have spent my entire time in China being escorted from meeting to meeting approved by the Communist Party and never had a chance to speak to a single woman in China about her experiences of her country, the world and her views

---

* At the end of the Chinese Communist Party's nineteenth Congress (2017, also the year I travelled to China) the new Politburo Standing Committee (the most powerful politicians in China) was made up of seven men. There has never been a female member of the Standing Committee. Of the 2,280 delegates at that Congress, fewer than a quarter were women. Only two of the twenty-five members of that Politburo were women – 8 per cent.

of the United Kingdom.* In each meeting, I continued to raise the question of what they did about domestic abuse and sexual violence in China. In financial meetings on China's investment in developing countries, after I had been told about their environmental sustainability goals in any investment, I would ask how they were making sure that their investments aided the women in these developing countries as well as the environment. What were their targets for women? Very few had any answers.

I understand that on such delegations I must be polite and act with courtesy to my host and I will always, without question, do so. But that does not mean I have to act like some sort of silent concubine who cannot raise questions, politely and persistently, about the issues that I care about – just as I do with the government of my own country.

It was very stark when we visited a charitable school set up for migrants on the outskirts of Beijing (not external to China migrants, but external to Beijing migrants, who could not access the school system in Beijing as easily as city residents). In every class, boys outnumbered girls, and in the nursery classes there were three or four girls to a class of twenty-odd

---

* I was in fact able to speak to many Chinese women in the less formal meetings and with charitable groups. However, I detected a sense of secrecy and privacy and an element of pride that meant these stopped short of some of the interactions I have had with citizens in other parts of the world. One young woman I met said she had seen footage of Jeremy Corbyn taking the micky out of Theresa May in Parliament, and other jokes and videos online of people laughing at the prime minister, and she thought it was really funny that we thought it was okay to ridicule our leaders. I have been all over the world and China is one of the nicest, safest, kindest, friendliest places I have been – but of all the countries I have visited, it is the one I could never live in, for the simple fact that too few people feel they can speak freely there. I am not suited to such a regime.

boys. A lag from an era of the one-child policy had clearly left girl children a rarity. It made me wonder how they would manage to hold up their equal portion of the sky.

On our final evening of a four-day trip in Beijing, where we had met government officials, visited schools and universities, dined with local British and Chinese staff at British businesses operating out of Beijing, studied the high-speed trains and spoken to British students in China and Chinese students who studied in Britain, we were once again invited back for a formal meeting and then a banquet at the Hall of the People in Tiananmen Square. After the formal meeting, where we dutifully asked questions of the assembled Communist Party officials, this time led by a senior and quite brilliant woman, we were walked through the still eerily quiet halls of this amazing place and into an even grander hall with a huge banqueting table down the middle, like the royal banquets you see in period dramas. Golden cutlery and perfect porcelain were laid out and each of the seven courses we ate was produced dramatically from under a golden cloche, as if in a French cartoon about a flamboyant chef.

The food was, I was told, a fusion of British and Chinese cuisine in honour of the meeting of minds. The Chinese food was delicious, as all of the Chinese food on the trip had been (and far more delicate than the food we call 'a Chinese' at home). The British courses, however, were some of the most entertaining meals I have ever been served. Imagine, if you will, sitting in a banqueting hall in a palace dripping with gold, lined with deep red swathes of curtains, rich, plush carpets and a table set fit for a king. A ballet of servers swirl around you like the magical domestic appliances in

Beauty and the Beast and course after course is presented with due fanfare. The main course arrives, beautifully dressed women reach in perfect synchronicity from behind your chair to place a golden dome in front of you. You wait in anticipation for what this next course will be, giddy with wine and expectation. As all forty people at the dinner have the golden coverings removed in unison, you look down at the homage to your nation's cuisine and see a tender-looking ox cheek in a deep, reduced gravy – delicious. And alongside it, that quintessentially British accompaniment: McCain Potato Smiles.

I absolutely love the thought that someone in the Politburo had Googled, 'What do British people eat?' and McCain Potato Smiles had come up. Personally, I would have preferred the classic potato waffle, if we're going down the reformed potato product route, but I am sated by a happy face. Perhaps this was a subtle slight on British cuisine, perhaps it was a genuine homage – either way, I could do nothing but chuckle with delight. I cannot say that I felt the same way when a quite delicious mousse ice cream desert was garnished with Skittles but, hey, perhaps that is a delicacy in some parts of the UK that I have missed out on, like chicken parmo in Teesside or laverbread in Wales.

Our handler from the Communist Party who had stayed with us throughout the trip was a lovely, kind and friendly man, who laughed much more than anyone else on the trip. As he handed me my papers before I boarded the plane home, he said to me, 'It has been a pleasure to meet you, I think you got your message across that you like women.' I didn't like to disappoint him and say, 'Not all of them, bab, I like and dislike women in equal measure to men. I just wish everyone else did.'

I think Mao was right that women hold up half the sky, it's just that for their half they get paid less, hurt more and are expected to do the grunt work without ever getting to the top job of Sky Director, and I am not sure that was what Mao had intended when he uttered those words. But hey, what do I know, I don't put Skittles on ice cream.

7

The Room Where it Happens: The UN

Over the six years of my parliamentary career, I have attended several of the annual Commission for the Status of Women conferences at the United Nations in New York. It is a huge event where the nations of the world gather for two weeks to hash out treaties and documents outlining how they can work towards improving the global lot of women and girls. It may sound as though it should be an easy task – surely everyone would agree that the educational, economic and human rights of girls and women should be protected, you might say. You would be very wrong.

There is almost no global agreement on many of the issues raised. Even the notion that women should have autonomy over their own bodies is deeply controversial in many countries.* Marriage is another sensitive area: it is a deeply political institution in lots of parts of the world and the rights of a

---

* Before you think I am pointing the figure at Saudi Arabia or deeply Catholic parts of South America, every single time I have attended the congress, the UK fell short on its ability to sign up to women's reproductive rights because, until last year, female UK citizens in Northern Ireland were not allowed to access abortions with any ease. It is still practically impossible today, as Covid has provided a perfect cover for a legislature that has been determined to stand in the way of a woman's right to choose.

husband over his wife or a father over his daughter cannot be questioned. So the commission is anything but straightforward and diplomats from every country spend weeks going through a policy document line by line, trying to agree on language that they can all take forward together.

If you think things happen slowly in UK politics then I would invite you to go and sit in the negotiating room of the UN for a day – or a month, if you want to see anything get done. At my first commission, on the first day, I joined the British team of negotiators in the congress room where the policy document was being discussed. After four hours, we were still quibbling over the first sentence in a document that stretches to hundreds of pages. That morning, I had a series of epiphanies. First, that I would make a terrible diplomat – I tutted very loudly every time Saudi Arabia's all-male team of representatives disagreed with anything. And second, I just don't have the patience for this kind of work. To be honest, it is a wonder that anything has ever been agreed at the UN when so many people from such varied cultures and with very different expectations are asked for their opinion. Bravo to the amazing people who have both the temperament and also the stamina, but I know my skill set and that is not it. I'm more of an 'act first, apologise later' kinda gal, more wrecking ball than gentle nudge.

My job at this convention, thankfully, was not to negotiate the finer points of a thousand-page document but to join with the hundreds of representatives from other nations of the world and development charities, meeting and lobbying and cajoling countries to agree to the things I wanted out of the negotiations. I am much more suited to having a drink, a yarn and a debate with the Equalities ministers from Italy and

New Zealand than I am to sitting for hours quibbling about where the comma goes or what is an acceptable phrase for enshrining the sanctity of a woman's womb.* This conference is also an opportunity to meet with other MPs from around the world and hear about successes they have had with, for example, sexual harassment legislation or changes to policy around domestic abuse. It is essentially like Davos or the G8 for women's rights and the reason you've probably never heard of it before is because who gives a toss about the plight of half the global population?

However, it is not only people like me who are there to lobby; some of those who are working the convention are there to lobby *against* advancing rights for lesbians or *against* a woman's right to choose, to file for divorce or just to think for herself. The most prolific lobbyists in this area, in my experience, are from the Holy See or, as some people call it, the Magisterium of the Supreme Pontiffs – the Vatican.

All around the conference centre you will see an army of young men with 'The Holy See' badges around their necks, working the room like holiday reps, looking for the delegates from Catholic countries who are likely to agree with the Vatican's approach to the negotiations. Fair play to them, they have just as much right to lobby for their opinions as I do. Although, actually, scrap that. I am not sure any young man

---

* If you would ever like to see a feminist woman about to explode, put her in a dark conference room and ask her to listen to loads of men talking about her reproductive organs and what they will and won't tolerate being said about them in global treaties. For my male readers, imagine sitting in a roomful of women while they discuss what you can and can't do to keep your penises healthy or how your testicles should be considered the property of another person.

has the same right as me, a woman and an elected representative, to push for what I should be allowed to do with my body. Unfortunately, in the eyes of the convention they *do* have as much right as me and so they are everywhere, lobbying for more conservative language to be adopted as the world tries to tackle the global exploitation of girls and women.

One year, I was speaking at a morning seminar on the need to provide good sex and relationship education to all children, everywhere, in order to instil an understanding of healthy, respectful, non-harmful relationships from a young age. Up pops the hand of a young American man emblazoned with the Holy See sash and he says to a very crowded hot room of women from around the world: 'I don't have children yet but if I did, I don't want them going to school to learn how to masturbate.' It was a slightly odd comment as none of the speakers had said anything about teaching kids to masturbate; the seminar had been about teaching about consent and respect and helping young people to understand the harm of gender norms in relationships. No one apart from this man had mentioned masturbation. I think he thought it would be too shocking or embarrassing to receive a rebuttal, but he did not bank on the fact that women have to discuss embarrassing things on a near-daily basis.

Female delegates from around the world did a massive collective eye roll. Politely and calmly, I responded from the stage, 'Thank you for your concern. No one is suggesting for a second what you have wrongly asserted; we are talking about keeping children safe from harm. However, as someone who does have children, let me tell you, there's no need to teach masturbation in school because they all learn by themselves and crack on with enthusiasm regardless, as I am sure you well know.' When I imagined being an elected representative, I had never expected to find myself talking about wanking at the UN, but here we were. However, the joke's on me in the end. Because while I am smarter and more capable of pontificating on sex and sex education in public without even the slightest blush, ultimately the more conservative language usually wins out at these events.

The Commission for the Status of Women takes place to coincide with International Women's Day on 8 March each year. This means I usually find myself in New York on St Patrick's day, on the seventeenth, and over the years have watched some MPs do some fairly heavy drinking followed by some fairly embarrassing dancing. However, in March 2018, all of this was somewhat upstaged by the poisoning of exiled Russian spy Sergei Skripal and his daughter Yulia in the picturesque and sleepy city of Salisbury.

Obviously, I had read about the incident on the news and was following the international relations fallout, as the UK government, backed by their European partners and the USA, accused Russia of perpetrating the killing of British citizens on British soil. My own political party, at the time headed up by Jeremy Corbyn, seemed to be merrily trying to avoid blaming Russia for the attack, with the consequence of appearing to the electorate as though Corbyn would back Russia over British intelligence. I don't think this was necessarily his intention but it was certainly the outcome.

While all of this was going on, I was running from meeting to meeting at the UN. But finding myself with an hour to spare, my colleague Gavin Shuker and I went to have a peek inside the room at the UN where the security council is held.

We wanted to see Picasso's famous *Guernica* painting and generally have a poke around the room we had seen many times on TV, where matters of war and peace are discussed by the nuclear powers of the world.

We walked in completely unimpeded and found a couple of other conference delegates milling around, taking pictures of the different countries' name plates around the famous circular table. It was quiet and still, and we sat down in the gallery just in front of the iconic scene for a few moments. Suddenly, a team of security staff came in, started checking everyone's passes and then ushered everyone out – with the exception of Gavin and me. I can only assume we were allowed to stay due to our British diplomatic passes. We were about to unexpectedly witness a special extra meeting of the security council, with the UK government poised to accuse fellow member of the security council Russia of an act of aggression on British soil.

In filed each of the powerful nation's representatives and their civil servants, translators and staff. We could see the press gallery filling up and realised we were about to have a front-row seat to history, though sadly not a landmark moment of peace but of a growing hostility between the nations of the UN security council. A piece of history I was going to witness by virtue of being a bit nosey and poking around in a room I shouldn't have been in.*

---

* I believe that the single most important attribute of a politician is to be nosey. I frequently want to find out more about people's lives, ask just one more question and generally get myself involved where people want to keep me out. Westminster thrives on gossip and it is literally my favourite pastime. I could dress this up as being professionally curious or interested in the lives of my constituents, but that would be the art of spinning. As my dad says, 'You're just a nosey bleeder.'

You can read the transcript of this meeting, during which the UK and US accused the Russian diplomats of what amounts to an act of war and started to talk about the banishment of Russian agents, ambassadors and diplomats from Britain and elsewhere. You can read how Russia denied it fiercely and essentially accused the UK and others of orchestrating the act themselves in order to frame Russia. (It was all somewhat reminiscent of being five years old, when your annoying sibling swears blind to your parents that *you* had started a fight with *them*, conveniently omitting that it was because they had been throwing a ball at your head for a solid twenty minutes.) You can read how Vassily Nebenzia, the Russian representative, said that the British police didn't know what they were doing, just like the hapless Inspector Lestrade in the Sherlock Holmes books. Nebenzia stated that what was now needed was for Sherlock himself to turn up, speaking as if Sherlock Holmes were a real person. He was behaving as if he was just a bloke down the pub gassing with a few mates, not one of Russia's leading operatives speaking at the security council of the United Nations.

The transcript is amusing to read – an almost satirical look at propaganda and hyperbole – amusing, that is, if you ignore the dangerous poisoning of two people by a foreign state actor in your homeland. However, the transcript alone does not do justice to the atmosphere of tension in the room.

Vassily Nebenzia sat at the security council table as if he owned the room. With each bizarre utterance he seemed to grow in stature. He conveyed his annoyance and disgust with all of his body, slapping his hands on the table. His voice was deep, his tone guttural, incendiary and aggressive towards my country, and it was a spectacle to watch. That is what my eyes were telling me, at least, but as Nebenzia spoke in Russian, every word of his speech was relayed to me by a very softly spoken English woman who sounded like Miss Marple. It is a very jarring thing to watch a man who looks like an angry Russian Kojak slagging off your country with the voice of a polite British woman.

I never thought when I was a little girl that one day I would be present in the room where significant global geopolitical incidences would occur. When I studied history at A Level and then at university, I never thought that when the history of my lifetime was written some of it might come from my own eyewitness accounts. It is an unusual feeling to watch history roll out in front of you, to watch tensions between nations escalate, to be in the room when the prime minister of your country tells the world that our lives will change forever for some economic, health or geopolitical reason. It doesn't feel like history when you are living through a terror attack in the building you are in, or when you watch a nation state deny poisoning and espionage in your land.

In the historically significant moments I have witnessed I always feel a sense of privilege and luck at being allowed in the room, even when the news is hard to hear and events are frightening to contemplate. Perhaps this comes from my upbringing, my social circle and the level of expectations someone like me was told to have – or, more significantly, *not* to have. The history I studied history at school didn't feature girls like me; when we were shown photographs of the historic 1945 Yalta Conference, there weren't any girls wearing short skirts with ill-conceived Mandarin symbol tattoos on their midriff; the artefacts we studied from the formation of the League of Nations in 1920 were a world apart from my own. Perhaps I expected my life to be part of the social and economic history about how cities formed and what jobs ordinary folks had, but I didn't expect to be part of the big boys' history.

In the moment you witness global politics, national crisis or terror, you stop all of the normal political processing that you do as a political animal; you stop thinking about the angles, the possible critique and the lines of enquiry and concern – that will all come later, on reflection of events. If you are a kid who didn't come from a long line of ambassadors, military men and political leaders, in those moments I have found that I become an observer of all the detail, as if my eyes are those of all the normal people who will one day want to know what happened. It feels like such an enormous privilege to be part of history, and while no one like me was present at the formation of the League of Nations, I have stood on the balcony of the United Nations smoking a fag with a French member of Parliament, working out together how we could better improve global responses to abortion.

8

Orgasms and Imaginary Boats: How Politics is Reported

'Teach schoolgirls about orgasms, says Labour MP' (*Guardian*).

'Schoolgirls must be taught about orgasms, says Labour MP Jess Phillips' (*Birmingham Mail*).

And my absolute favourite of all: 'Girls as young as 11 should learn about ORGASMS says Labour MP who lives in "naked house"' (*Daily Star*).*

A quick Google revealed that no fewer than ten national newspapers had run almost identical stories that week in November 2018. It all stemmed from a podcast interview I'd given, which had then been written up in *Grazia* magazine, about the need to talk to girls about enjoying sex and about orgasms, rather than just terrifying them with the prospective of an unwanted pregnancy. I like to think of myself as the leading politician in the field of orgasms. Someone has got to do it.

* I made a comment in the podcast interview that I come from the kind of family where people walk around naked. We are not the sort who wear pyjamas or are worried about getting changed in front of others. We are not naturists, just lazy. If I need a wee in the middle of the night, I am going to walk to the bathroom naked.

I was asked to appear on almost all of the major UK news networks to talk about the issue and, if memory serves, a couple of US publications also contacted me. I was not able to respond to any of these requests as I was in China at the time and didn't have access to any Western media. Nor did I have my phone with me, for security reasons, so I was blithely unaware that I was trending in the UK talking about orgasms. The first time I heard about it was on the plane on my way home from Beijing, when a woman flagged me down as I queued for the loo, held up a newspaper showing my face with 'Orgasm' emblazoned across it and shouted, 'Is this you? Bloody bravo.'

The spreading of a story in this manner is a phenomenon I still fail to either understand or manage. When I made the comments so salaciously reported across the media, I was not writing a policy paper on the issue of sex education, I was not taking part in a debate in the House of Commons or even speaking about the topic on the news. I have, on many occasions, spoken on this topic in my professional role; I have written relationship education programmes for the Home Office, for example, on helping children to avoid sexual exploitation and about gender norms that lead to domestic abuse. In fact, I am something of an expert in the field of healthy relationship education and have spoken about it extensively and, along with my fellow campaigners, managed to change the law to make it compulsory. I have, professionally, said many, many things on the topic of sex and relationship education that have not been reported and have struggled to be heard.

What I should have done in order to bring the subject to prominence was just talk about ejaculating. Seems that's where all the attention is. When I made these comments about women's orgasms, I was being interviewed on a feminist podcast called the Hotbed Collective. I did not *proffer* my opinion on women being taught about pleasure; during an informal podcast chat, I was asked: 'Do you think it's important to teach about pleasure?' Podcasts are very chatty and informal; I wasn't writing policy or proposing amendments to legislation, I was having a chat with a fellow woman about how crappy our own sex education had been growing up and how the epidemic of domestic and sexual violence is linked to a bad system whereby girls are essentially taught that sex will make you sick with an unpronounceable disease or will immediately put a baby in your belly. We have been trying to scare the shit out of kids to stop them having sex for generations. Guess what? People are still having sex. The Victorian approach is not working. Perhaps if we taught young women that they should be active, willing and equal participants in sexual encounters, that they should expect to enjoy it, not just tolerate it, then maybe – just maybe – we could shift some of the sexual power away from men and onto women.

In the interview, I actually say, 'You just know the *Daily Mail* is going to write this up as "Jess Phillips wants to teach masturbation to five-year-olds".' (They didn't, although I think this was largely because I had called them out. They were pretty fair, all things considered – although they did include the somewhat irrelevant occupation of my ten-years-deceased mother.) I was clearly aware of the possibility that this story would be picked up.

The trouble is not how I feel about this but how it is perceived by the public who don't hear the original interview but do see the subsequent out-of-context headlines, tweets or Facebook posts. Because of my position as an MP, it may appear as though I was proposing new legislation or a policy platform, rather than what it was: just two feminists chewing the fat about various things that might improve the lot of women in the future. I also made a cake on *Celebrity Bake Off* that said 'Smash the Patriarchy' in butter icing, but there were no headlines suggesting that I was proposing a complete policy overhaul of male-dominated institutions. I guess, as they say, sex sells – and the word 'orgasm' does look good in print splashed (excuse the pun) across the face of a female politician.

I use this example because I think it speaks to a particular trend in how political media operates in the UK: the phenomenon of 'committing news'. It is important to note that you can commit news quite easily and accidentally by saying anything that is vaguely interesting and not totally scripted. I like to think of myself as quite a sparky character who speaks to people not just as a politician but also as an interested equal. As a result, I have a tendency to let my guard down in most situations – as was the case with the interviewer on this podcast. Some may call it thoughtless, but I was just honest and spoke to her as I would a friend or colleague. Of course, this is a disastrous policy if you are trying not to commit news. One of the problems is that I have absolutely no idea when I am speaking what will be picked up by the press or not. Unfortunately, given my chosen profession, I have no radar for it.

You are not supposed to go too far off script in politics. There are teams of professionals working with politicians, prepping them before every interview and honing the exact message that they want to land. Listen out and you'll notice that there is often a number thrown in – one that sounds big to an ordinary punter but which is in fact just a cover for the truthful statistic, which is that not enough is being done. A good example of this during the Covid-19 crisis was when the Education Secretary (who, by the way, I would not allow to be any sort of secretary; he would unquestionably be incapable of filing things in alphabetical order) announced that 1,500 members of the armed forces would be drafted in to undertake testing in England's schools. To the average parent that sounds as if uniformed men and women with good manners and discipline are about to descend on their children's school to save the day with military efficiency. In reality, there are 3,300 secondary schools in England, not even counting primary schools, so that's not quite half a member of the military per school. In reality, each school was going to get a one-hour webinar from military personnel who would never actually set foot in the school. But that's not the message that the Education Secretary was interested in putting out. Clever, eh?

In any interaction with the press, a politician will usually have a message that they want to, or have been told to, land. This is why politicians generally don't answer the question put to them, much to the public's increasing irritation, and instead do whatever they can to stick to the pre-prepared message. As much as the public might hate it, this isn't necessarily a bad thing: message discipline is actually quite necessary in order to properly and successfully communicate with the public. However, I am terrible at this. Absolutely useless.

When I am asked to go on the news and talk about a specific issue, say a brutal domestic homicide, or a factory closure in my constituency, I can focus on the message I want to get across and I can do it passably. Just passably. However, in more general interviews or at events where I am talking in public on broader issues, like feminism, politics, the Labour Party or the day's events in Westminster, I tend to be chattier, more convivial and less likely to toe the party line. This means that I commit news all the time without ever expecting it.

While this might be the case in my professional life, my private self is not newsworthy at all, however. I am happily married and have been my whole adult life; I don't scam money for fancy holidays; I recycle and to the best of my knowledge I have never accidentally or on purpose invited a terrorist for tea. I try not to share platforms with fascists, dictators or raging racists (though I do have to share a platform with other members of Parliament all the time). In other words, I am personally neither newsworthy nor scandalous (apart from occasionally sleeping in the nude in my own home – pretty racy). I tend to commit news simply by voicing on a public stage the kind of things that women are saying to each other over a cup of tea or in the women's bogs up and down the country.

Which is how I end up on record saying things like, 'Blokes in the Labour Party can be just as sexist as blokes in the Conservative Party.' Which is true. But of course the headlines read: 'Well-meaning left-wing men are the actual worst' (*I News*) and 'Left wing men are "the worst" Labour MP blasts as she slams Corbyn's industrial strategy' (*Express*) and 'Labour MP Jess Phillips: Left-wing men are "literally the worst" sexists'. Once again, this was not the message I intended to communicate.

This happened when I was at the Edinburgh Book Festival

and a woman in the audience asked me a direct question. Her voice and body language were heavy with what was clearly her own bitter experience when she asked if I thought that the political left were any better than the right when it came to sexism. I could have probably answered in a less pithy and clear way that would have not lent itself quite so easily to headlines but that would have been far less engaging for the audience, who want me to be honest, clear, authentic and normal.

Perhaps I will never understand how the press works because even though I have seen it make headlines, I still don't think that saying girls should be told about orgasms and that there is sexism in the left wing of politics qualifies as breaking news. If, however, I had said sex education should be better and more realistic and my statement meant it was going to change, that something was going to happen, then that might constitute news. If only! But the truth is, despite the fact that it is always implied by these headlines that I am somehow going to make sure the country bends to my every whim, I cannot even get my husband and children to do that. So you are probably safe from the Jess Phillips naked household decree that I am apparently mere moments away from launching.

My concern is that in their desperate search for a bit of drama, some of these headlines give the wrong impression. I do not think that left-wing men are 'the actual worst'. And I am not doing a speaking tour around the country about the female orgasm. Responding to the question probably took up less than five seconds of my day, while most of the rest of it will have been spent dealing with decidedly unorgasmic things like bins, drop kerbs, homeless families and sitting on statutory instrument committees on naval regulations. I get it, that stuff is not very interesting – unlike whether or not I wear pyjamas to bed. But it can be tiring when you are in the middle of wading through work to change the family courts system and you're receiving hundreds of phone calls about something you said about shagging at a charity comedy night. You can very quickly, and quite wrongly, become defined by these innocuous and out-of-context comments, when they represent almost nothing to do with your actual work as an MP.

I will no doubt continue to commit news because of how I communicate and I am okay with that because it means that my voice can be heard in the media. And in the cases of improving sex education and tackling sexism in the political left, these are issues I care about a lot (perhaps not so much the naked household decree). A mistake I do not make anymore, but that I made all the time when I was first elected, is to allow a journalist to use my name as a hook to hang any old story on. This happens to pretty much all MPs on a near-daily basis. A journalist will call you while you are running from one meeting to the next and ask you, 'Hey, what do you think about the news that [insert obscure not-news-story of choice]?'* You very often have zero strong feelings about the matter. Contrary to popular belief, there are many things I have absolutely no strong feelings about: Buckingham Palace,

---

* A lot of this stuff these days comes from Twitter because politicians today feel that if anything happens, anywhere in the whole wide world, their constituents will hate them if they don't have an immediate opinion and express it in 280 characters.

what bank holidays should be in memory of, what happens if Big Ben stops chiming while it is being refurbished, pretty much most royal stories,* any stories about the naming of boats or the merry-go-round of people being granted or stripped of their titles. There are people where I live who are dying while waiting to be told whether they are ill enough to receive disability benefits and every week I handle cases of rape and child abuse; I will find the bandwidth to have deep feelings about knighthoods when I've dealt with those issues.

Having said that, there is a reciprocal professional relationship between politicians and lobby journalists, and even if you have no strong feelings on the matter, sometimes you can feel them crashing towards a deadline and so you do them a favour and come up with a few lines to help them out. After all, it will only be line twenty-two in the text of a story on page five. Well . . . not always. Sometimes, unbeknownst to you, the quote you gave on Big Ben chiming, or the new bloody statue of Mrs Thatcher, becomes the story. Instead of your name just being a dull, incidental part of a broader issue, the headline reads: 'Labour MP calls for the government to halt bank holiday dedicated to divisive Iron Lady'.

In this instance, the half-arsed quote that you came up with while running up a flight of stairs and thinking about three

---

* Not Prince Andrew. I have some pretty strong feelings about him. When I initially swore my oath to the queen and all her heirs, which all MPs have to do in order to take their seats in the House of Commons, I crossed my fingers. Not because I hate the royal family (I'm quite fond of the queen), but because I didn't want to pledge allegiance to Prince Andrew. Even back in 2015, before his car-crash interview about his inability to sweat in a Pizza Express in Woking, I was not keen. My dad assured me that a terrible tragedy would have to befall the royal family before I end up acting out an allegiance to Andrew and so I was probably safe.

other things is the hook that the journalist needed to make a story run. Writing about the bank holiday naming in and of itself might not have filled the space, but if you have someone saying something even mildly controversial about it, then it will. This story will then be written up three more times and to the public it starts to look as though you have called the media to a press conference to make a speech launching your anti-Thatcher bank holiday campaign, when in reality it was a phone call saying, 'Surely, Jess, you don't want a Thatcher Day?' To which you responded, 'Er, yeah, go on then, I am not that bothered but loads of people who suffered under Thatcher would probably consider it a betrayal so perhaps we should find someone less divisive to have a bank holiday for.'*

Stories like these ones need a personality in order to make them newsworthy and unfortunately lots of politicians, including myself, have newsworthy names. I remember a rather drunken diary columnist† coming up to me and exclaiming, 'Jess, you are just such brilliant copy, you make my job easy!' My husband, who unusually was with me at a London event, said, 'Bab, I'm not sure that was a compliment.'

---

* This is a fictitious example. Having learned from previous experience, when I really was asked if Lady Thatcher should have a bank holiday in her name, I gave the unsatisfactory answer that I couldn't give a toss. If it meant we were going to get an extra day off work they could call it whatever they liked. (It was not extra in the end; it was just renaming an existing one, which is so very Mrs Thatcher, to be remembered for not giving anything extra.) My quote didn't make it into the copy as it did not fit the role the press have cast me in.

† I was not aware that this was a thing before I was elected to Parliament but there are people employed just to go to parties and book launches. Their job is to get entertaining titbits, usually from drunk people. I had obviously read various accounts like this in papers and magazines before I was elected but for some reason it had never occurred to me that finding out party gossip was an actual *job*. I would love that job.

The young journalist had meant it as one but my husband is quite right. It can be a real chore being lumped with positions on issues you don't care that much about, especially when people start reacting to the story and attacking you from all sides. Before you know it, a story you don't even care about is being touted as your current and most pressing concern and will no doubt be referred to many years into your future whenever anyone writes anything about you. 'Jess Phillips, famous advocate against Mrs Thatcher's bank holiday, has died today at the ripe age of 89.'

It is the same phenomenon that leads the public to thinking that MPs are all busy talking about their own pay or how the taxpayer should buy the queen a new yacht. One MP will say something in a speech or put down an Early Day Motion about how important it is for the morale of the nation for a new royal yacht to be commissioned, and the headline reads, 'MPs have debated plans for a new royal yacht today, exploring how to fund a replacement vessel' (*City AM*). The headline is not untruthful – yes, a debate did happen in Westminster about a royal yacht – but it is misleading. The reality is that it was a backbench debate called by a backbencher with literally zero chance of getting the thing he was asking for; there will have been about six MPs in the debate, which will have lasted maybe an hour, max. Not to mention the fact that, in this instance, the minister's response to the idea of aid money (money for the poorest parts of the world) being spent on a new boat for the queen was a firm and resounding 'no'.

It was a nothing event in Westminster. It will do absolutely nothing to change anything in our country. But it is a good story and so it was written about everywhere. 'Tory MP plans to fund a new royal yacht slammed as an affront to struggling British families' (*I News*). 'These MPs just debated buying the Queen a royal yacht instead of the brutal civil war in Syria' (*Mirror*). I read about that bloody boat debate over and over again, and countless people tweeted me about it. For a while, you could believe that the only thing being debated in Parliament was a bloody boat that isn't even a boat but just an idea of a boat to have in the future. It is no wonder that people start to hate politicians. By all means take a pop at the Yachty McYachtface ones, but the way these stories appear makes it seem as if Westminster is a callous place full of callous people who care more about imaginary boats than they do about the lives and livelihoods of ordinary British people.

I just wish I could sub-edit these stories with the real-istic facts:

'Today a debate was held in Parliament. Only six out of 650 MPs attended, giving an idea of the level of national interest in the subject matter. The subject in question was proposed by an MP with a hobby horse about the state funding a new royal yacht to travel around the world. The MP was told in no uncertain terms by the government minister in charge that there wouldn't be a new royal yacht commissioned. Almost all other MPs who voted with their feet by not attending the debate sent a clear message that it was probably best not to have a new boat because, as a country, we have quite a lot on our plates at the minute. One backbench Labour MP said, 'Maybe we could think about a boat for the queen, which, by the way, she hasn't asked for, when we have sorted out child poverty and the lack of funding for our armed forces.'

Both versions of the story are factually accurate. The journo's version will get a lot of clicks but will also, unfortunately, give the entirely wrong impression. I have read accounts of party political meetings that I have attended that sound so thrilling and dramatic when committed to paper. In fact, I was so bored in said meeting I started playing Peggle on my phone. When it comes down to it, the boat story is essentially: man said something in fancy building that is unlikely to come to pass.

The problem with these stories is that they misdirect public attention away from the important work that MPs are doing. I checked my diary for the day this debate took place: 11 October 2016. On this date, I arrived at the Southbank Centre over the river from Parliament at 7 a.m. and spent the first three hours of my day mentoring girls aged eleven to fifteen for the International Day of the Girl. I talked one-to-one with many young women, listening to their hopes and dreams and giving them advice and possible useful contacts. At 11 a.m., I returned to Parliament where I took calls with constituents, including assisting a young man in making a complaint to the police against a man who had abused him as a child.

After lunch, along with many other members of Parliament, I joined Alison McGovern MP in the Commons debate calling for support for Syrian Opposition plans against the barrel bombing in Aleppo. On that day, Alison took up the mantle of Jo Cox, who had been killed only months beforehand and who had spent much of her career fighting for refugees and all of her political career fighting for support for Syrians who were being massacred by their rulers. Alison wept in her speech, in memory of her murdered friend and at the horrors suffered by the people of Aleppo.

A shit tonne of good work will have been done on that day; a heap load of humanity and care will have been shown. MPs in their offices will have interacted with hundreds if not thousands of ordinary people on that day and tried to help them with their various problems. But the boat is the thing folks will remember.

I can hear the response from various journalists echoing in my head: 'Look, if you don't want us to write about the stupid stuff you lot say, then don't say it.' They have a point. If people could stop asking for royal boats, I would be grateful. We all say stupid things and it is part of the role of the press to keep us in check. But unfortunately, it can lead to MPs either obsessing over what might potentially blow up into a story and consequently not getting anything done or, as in the case of the sodding boat, certain types of MP calling for something they know they are never going to get and using the guaranteed media attention to their advantage. In other words, this kind of press coverage favours boring, cautious politicians or ones who will seek to manipulate it. Neither is good.

Boring politicians don't engage the people – and sometimes this is a shame. I can see an argument at the moment for a bit of boring after the Boris, Brexit, Trump, Putin years. Unfortunately, we can find ourselves in something of a catch-22 situation. If we do and say nothing beyond the script, people will disengage in desperate boredom. But the entertaining stories can make the public think we are all a load of bell/clock tower/boat/knighthood/castle-obsessed toffs, which also disengages people. Politics is essentially really dull but necessary bureaucracy that has a sideline in drama and intrigue. Unfortunately, neither particularly screams 'We are here to serve' or 'Politics is for the people'.

My relationship with the media is largely a good and co-productive one. I am good for a quote and they are keen to write about and film my campaigns and the issues that I care about. We need to find a balance where we politicians can be firmly held to account by the press for our inevitable stupidity, while at the same time the press more fairly highlight all that politics is and does. We don't currently have that equilibrium and so most people wrongly think that the majority of politicians have their hands in the till, never do any work and don't give a stuff about the regular citizen. I have to say that I think I have been lucky, or have managed the media well, as I don't think the public at large think these things about me – but in this I am too often considered to be an exception when actually I am the rule.

We need to find a way to better invite people into the *work* of politics, not just the game of politics, because the game is far more off-putting to the public. The work of politics is genuine graft for the betterment of our country. Usually, the only time a politician is given public credit for this is when they are eulogised. I cannot stress enough that the fastest way for democracy to decline is for the public to disengage through cynicism and exasperation, and the media bears huge responsibility here. The way that politics works with today's media needs to find a new groove for the benefit of everyone.

9

Pls Like: Politics and Social Media

In recent years, the already hyper media cycle has stepped up a notch. Journalists are no longer trying to come up with a new story each day but now every hour or so. Content races past, tweets become news and everything moves so fast that you can be in and out of a media storm by the time you sit down for your dinner in the Commons tearoom at 7 p.m. This can make it harder than ever to ensure your views are accurately reported in the press – before you get a chance to respond, the world has moved on.

Very early on in my political career, I got annoyed with the things being written about me that misrepresented my actual views. So I decided to write for newspapers and online blogging sites about the kind of job I do. I got to control what was said. I got to write about the people coming into my office in Birmingham. I got to share my opinion, which might be nuanced and careful or it might be very bloody strident, but I got to write it without one quote being pulled out and over-dramatised.*

While I still do this, these days we have a more direct route to the public. Enter social media, stage left. More and more, you see politicians using social media to tell the story of their day, week, month in politics. Video content in particular is becoming more popular. There are some notable examples of people who do this extremely well. In the US, they are unsurprisingly lightyears ahead, with people like Alexandria Ocasio-Cortez streaming videos of her chopping veg in her kitchen while she explains the legislation she had been working on that day to viewers, breaking down the complicated legislature while moving around her kitchen as if the viewer is just over at hers for a cuppa and a chat. It's very clever. I have no idea how successful it is in telling the actual story of the legislation, but it cannot hurt.

Here in the UK, we are still catching up, and for most politicians, the use of social media and video content is still limited to 'politician in front of building wearing hard hat pointing'. So far, all we've really seen are the old leaflet images of politicians indicating potholes in the road† brought to life in a shaky phone video. We have yet to advance to

---

* With the exception of the goddamn headline. Yes, I get to control what I write when I write opinion pieces for newspapers, and this is a benefit – however, I do not get to write the headline, and in a world of social media this is all most people read, so a misleading headline can attribute a view to me that I don't really have, did not express in the piece and which makes people furious. But hey, this is a hazard I am too small to solve.

† Part of my constituency is called Sheldon. One of the local councillors there is on pretty much every leaflet squatting down pointing at a pothole; the position he adopts looks like he is defecating, which has led us to call this series of leaflets 'Shitting on Sheldon'.

truly interactive social media where the public feel that it is a conversation rather than merely a broadcast of something that is either dull or a bit propaganda-y.

I remain unconvinced that big set-piece speeches that are written up by the media are effective in reaching the public. Yes, they make headlines and push out political messages, but do people actually watch them outside of times of crisis? I don't, and I am a massive political nerd. I am much more interested in having a real, live conversation with the people, and I think that this might be the key to how we improve the standing of politics in people's daily lives.

Like most of my colleagues, I've still got a long way to go on this front. How I use social media and the content that I write is without doubt a bit broadcasty; I am not here to say I am an engagement genius and that I have never been photographed stood in front of a school or community centre. I have, every day and twice on Sundays. However, what I try to do in any content is to elevate the voices of the people involved, to write about their stories, use them in the videos (the pandemic has been an absolute pain in the bum for this) and to feature conversations between us.

When I am putting out communications, I always keep a woman called Brenda in my head. Brenda is an invented character (although she definitely exists and one day I *will* find her). Brenda works in Asda in Birmingham, she is in her fifties and has a couple of grown-up kids and a new grandchild. Brenda came into my life during the #MeToo movement when I was spending quite a lot of time on the phone to the women in California who were tasked with setting up the Time's Up sexual harassment fund in the

UK. We were trying to work out the best way to roll out a scheme to assist women in the UK who were being sexually harassed in their workplace. How could we speak to these women? How could we get support to them? Throughout the process, I was sat in my house in Birmingham, talking to lots of women with high-level fancy jobs and even fancier friends, and my whole job became exclaiming at the end of every suggestion, 'Can we remember Brenda in the local Asda? How is this going to help her?' or 'Do we think Brenda would be able to access this service?' Brenda is my lodestar. Whenever anything is suggested to me in policy, and especially when we talk about political communication and how to reach people, I think of Brenda and I wonder if this message or this idea would get to her.*

I use my different social media platforms for different purposes. I use Facebook to talk about local issues and what I am doing as the MP for the area I serve. This is largely because Facebook geolocates far better than other platforms. On Instagram, I am just Jess, I am not an MP; I take selfies of good eye make-up and bits of my house I have curated to look nice, just like every other narcissist on there. Obviously, there is some political content because I am a politician and my daily life is political, just like a train driver might post images or videos of their journeys or their cab, but mostly it's my kids' Lego and my girlfriends dancing. I think it is important to show that I live a normal life, that I get sweaty when I am dancing, sometimes (shock horror) I get drunk,

---

* In my head, Brenda and I get on like a house on fire. We have a proper giggle together, although both of us roll our eyes at the other one because we have wildly differing views on many things. Brenda hates garlic.

sometimes I think my husband looks fit. And on occasion I'll post an image of me in the House of Commons because I think it's a great pic. But as everyone is aware, and as is the case for all Instagram users, it's all curated. It is a political act and a political choice to be 'just Jess' on this platform and to pretend otherwise would be disingenuous.

Twitter is the place where I am overly political, party political – and also human. Twitter is where I place my opinions on things in the full expectation of having a conversation on them – which I am very willing to do. And I will talk to people who both agree and disagree with me. There is both a humanising and dehumanising element to Twitter. It makes me genuinely closer to the people I'm having a direct conversation with. But at the same time, and it is a problem found across the internet, online anonymity means that sometimes people will forget that the person they are trolling/abusing is another human being on the far side of the computer screen. As someone who has spent many hours writing police statements and preparing for court cases because people have threatened to kill me online, I can testify to the dehumanising effect of internet communications.

It is my experience that the world we navigate online acts to dehumanise *all* the players. I use the term 'players' because to me it feels very much like a dopamine-driven game, where likes and shares are the mushrooms that make us bigger and where blue ticks are the elite who know the cheat codes. Now, when I stamp on a troll, I am Mario stamping on Bowser's head, but of course to some people *I* am Bowser. I am the boss baddie who must stamped on three times and thrown into the lava. Through the lens of social media, politics often becomes a no-win game of goodies and baddies, where everyone thinks that they are Mario and Luigi and the people who disagree with them are the Koopa Troopas. Politics is not a game, it is about real people and real lives. Politics online, however, is one big tournament.

I realised how dehumanising it had all become when the online battle smashed its way into my real life. On 26 September 2018, a man called Michael tried to kick in the door of my office while aggressively shouting insults at my staff and some of my constituents who were inside.* I was in Westminster at the time and received a phone call from my staff telling me that they had called the police and locked themselves in as there was a man shouting and screaming outside who was trying to smash the glass.

This was all too much for me. I stood outside the Palace of Westminster, on the phone to my terrified staff, and I started to cry. I felt guilty that I had put them in harm's way. I felt guilty that I had put my family in harm's way.

The man banging at the window of my office was calling me a fascist and exclaiming that I was blocking democracy. After the police had charged him and the story had become public, they printed his full name and address in the paper. When I read this, the man who had previously been a faceless

* We were also interviewing for a new constituency caseworker, so as well as my staff and two really vulnerable constituents locked in the office, there were also two people being interviewed for a job and one who had been stopped from attending their interview by the fray. Great advertisement for coming to work with me.

thug became a human being. Michael was the same age as me, he lived a few streets away from where I had grown up and he had gone to the same school as friends of mine. As soon as I saw this, I knew that our paths must have crossed before and I knew that if I met him I would be able to find common ground with him and try to understand why he had done what he did. So I got in touch with the police handling the case and I asked to meet him, to undertake what we call restorative justice and explain to him how he had made me feel and to listen to what he had to say in return.

So a few weeks after the incident I met with Michael at my local police station and I asked him why he had wanted to attack me and my office. He told me that he had read online that I hated people like him and I had said that people who voted for Brexit were thick. He told me he had read online that I had turned a blind eye to grooming gangs. I spent an hour or so with Michael and I told him that we had come from the same streets and that he had gone to the same school as my husband. We reminisced about our childhood neighbourhood, the old BMX track now long gone, the crappy nightclubs in town in the 1990s. Michael realised that I was 'people like him'.

Setting the record straight, I showed him a video of a speech that I made to a million people who had marched for a people's vote on Brexit, where I explicitly said, 'I ask you all never to ever treat my constituents who voted for Brexit as if they are stupid.' Beamed all over big screens on London I told a crowd of passionate Remainers that the people who voted Brexit wanted what was best for Britain, just like they did. On the grooming gangs, I told Michael about the years I had spent setting up services for groomed children in the midlands. I showed him the book I had written about the whistleblowers who fought for the girls in Rochdale who had been groomed by a gang of British Asian men. I explained to him that what he had been told about me online was not true; it was all part of a divisive game where someone pretending to be Mario told Michael that I was Bowser and that he should try to stamp on my head. People who pretended to represent 'people like' Michael without knowing him acted to dehumanise me and make him believe that I was worthless, that I was a symbol not a human. People who claimed to care about 'people like him' had wound him up and harmed him: they landed him in court, he lost his job and now has a criminal record.

Michael is a man who thinks differently to me on many things and he is a man who still gets in touch when he needs help with stuff, or if he is cross about something he has seen. I reply to him, we have a debate, and when we can meet again after the pandemic I have no doubt we will have gentle-to-robust conversations in my office. Michael is a human being just like me. He is not an internet avatar and I am not a video game baddy he must stamp on. But online worlds sometimes smash into real-life worlds, and there are consequences.

A politician's own social media channels can, to some extent, provide a balance to the skewed online portrayals. However, there is an obvious downside to politicians breaking out of mainstream media* and telling their own

---

* People use the shorthand MSM to refer derisively to the mainstream media and I was honestly confused the first time I saw it used. Thanks to my years working in sexual health education I thought it meant Men who have Sex with Men, as that is the abbreviation for that in that field.

story in the growing online political environment, and that is that they will curate it to be flattering to them. Political journalists, both the good and bad ones, provide checks and balances because they are free from the need to promote a politician or a party line. Now, this is obviously bullshit, to some extent, as lots of journalists will like, respect and agree with certain politicians and so give them a more favourable write-up. But within the wider picture of mainstream journalism I think it is safe to say that (stories about royal bloody yachts aside) you're likely to receive a fuller picture than the one that a two-minute video clip on Twitter of a rousing speech or question can imply.

Our video-clip-sharing era is changing politics massively and does not, in my view, tend to enlighten anyone as to what happens in our legislature. In Parliament, you can sometimes see that people are speaking only to get their weekly two-minute clip for the website. Prime Minister's Questions is dogged by the fact that both sides have to grab that one-minute, rabble-rousing, hand-thumping moment for Facebook and Twitter. But when viewing that brief clip online, you will never see the full picture of the debate – where the prime minister might have agreed with the statement (okay, this rarely happens) or where, along the way, consensus broke out. But the popularity of these clips means that MPs do exactly the same thing that journalists do: they follow the story. They think about the clicks and the likes. So even this new world of sharing and apparent transparency does not properly allow the public into the reality of the legislature of our country. It is broadcast and broadcast alone.

Now, I feel like I am being terribly negative about the media, both on and offline. Perhaps I am just bellyaching about a problem I cannot see my way through. I cannot fathom a solution that would really open up our politics and lend proper transparency so that people could feel part of it and in charge of it. I guess the onus is on all the players to sign up to a principle of responsible and transparent reporting.

There are already undoubtedly positives. For the most part, I choose to focus on the smooth over the rough and to see my ability to interact with the public through social media as a positive in the democratisation of the political process. Though, of course, there is plenty of proof and reams of literature that you can and should read on how social media is manipulated to change democracy – the Cambridge Analytica scandal is always a good place to start. Then there is the upswing in the online promotion of conspiracy theories in American politics around the time of the Trump–Clinton presidential race, which has led to the QAnon phenomenon and seen some of the followers of these bizarre theories elected to the US Congress. The online and real-world implications for politics are, for better or worse, inextricably intertwined. And politics will have to learn to work with that.

Twitter, Facebook and TikTok, and whatever comes next, have the potential to make politics far more accessible. The trouble is that there is no money or power in democratising the internet and so the various states and multi-billion-dollar companies are not interested in investing the time and energy in this. What can I say? Power doesn't want ordinary folks feeling empowered; it wants them feeling fearful, reactionary and controlled. What we need is for a tech billionaire, or rich nation state, to actually *want* the Internet to become a genuinely democratising force for good in our politics – but I wouldn't hold your breath. It is unlikely that the Russian bot farms will be replaced by warehouses full of people trying to set up community action online any time soon.

10

'It's Complicated': How Journalists and Politicians Really Get On

I cannot complain too much because the way I interact with the media and with the political landscape has made a pretty solid career for me. I am relatively comfortable in both environments and I am able to have a foot in both camps. It is important to say here that media and communications are not the same as journalism. Opinion is not the same as journalism. There is even a difference between reportage and really good deep-dive political journalism and it is in the latter that I think hope lies. Proper, good journalism, undertaken in Westminster is as important as any of the other players in the building. The media are as vital as the parliamentary representatives because they are our link to the people.

There is a tussle between lobby journalists and politicians about who is *really* the voice of the people. I can't count the number of times lobby journalists have said to me, 'This is what our readers think and care about' when I have rolled my eyes at the way something has been represented in the press. Similarly, I have lectured what can be a very London-centric political journalism class with the sarcastic line, 'Yes, the good people of Birmingham Yardley speak of little else than the Northern Ireland protocol.' Politicians and lobby journalists are forever in a chicken–and–egg situation where it's never quite clear who is setting the agenda: do politicians respond to what gathers media interest (yes); do the media write about the politician's interest (yes, within reason). Both are true. Politicians and journalists are like a two–headed snake where one cannot function without the other but on both sides there is a slight feeling of superiority and advanced righteousness.

When it comes to the individuals involved, it's more complicated. I genuinely couldn't do my job without really solid mutually respectful relationships with political writers, producers and broadcasters. However, if you were to use a Facebook status to describe the relationship between politicians and political journalists in general, it would definitely be 'it's complicated'. The public's view of the relationship between newspapers and politicians tends to be polarised: they either think we hate each other or that politicians are all too pally and cosy with media moguls and reporters in order to get good coverage. As far as I am concerned, neither is accurate; it is in fact a far more functional, mundane and professional relationship.

Let's start by covering the formalities of relationships with political journalists. First, we all work in the same building as each other. Too often the representation of journalism on the telly is reporters in raincoats standing outside government buildings or an MP's house, begging for them to respond to a question. This is very misleading. We are colleagues who walk the same corridors, eat the same food, drink in the same pubs and often have the same interests and concerns. We ask about each other's kids just as you might with Colin from accounting who works on a different floor to you but whom you often bump into in the staff car park. We sit in the same canteen areas and have our lunch together. I have queued for a coffee behind the political editors of the BBC and ITN more times than I could count. We are not mortal enemies, however it might appear in the press. Journalists who have written horrendous (and I would argue unfair) things about me have leant over to ask if they can have the salt cellar off my table in the canteen and followed it up with incidental chat about the weather. People have occasionally apologised to me for things that others at their publication have said about me, but by and large it is just part of the job. Portcullis House is not like an American high school where I stop people sitting near me at lunch because I saw them looking at my boyfriend. It is a workplace.

Can you ever really be friends with the journalists who are there to scrutinise you? The answer is yes, of course you can, because they are human beings too and you will naturally build a relationship with some of them, as with any other colleague in your workplace. When you do become friends with a journalist, there is a strong possibility that one day they will be called on to write a potentially harmful story about you, and you have to accept that not as a betrayal but as a hazard of your job. I would of course expect them to be completely fair and balanced in their approach, and I would be likely to receive a fair warning and a chance to put across my side. But if you had been caught with your hands in the till, pants down or thumbs up to wrong'uns then you would have to accept it. If you expected that friendship to mean your wrongdoing was safe from criticism, then I would argue that, on your part, the friendship wasn't real but was for your convenience.

I have made friends with a number of political journalists in my time in Westminster. I know that if I told them a personal secret and asked them not to share it, they wouldn't. I have done this. I can also think of six separate occasions when journalists have approached me for help, either personally or for a member of their family or a friend who is suffering from domestic abuse or sexual violence. I have helped people go to court, leave their homes, make police complaints and generally been a support to those whom a swathe of the public assumes I hate and distrust. I have celebrated birthdays and the births of children with them. There are many for whom I would drop everything I was doing to help.

You're probably now thinking the opposite: we are too close and the personal aspects of our relationships mean that they would never be able to critique me professionally as journalists – and yet they do. I think my ability to build a relationship with any group of people will always pay dividends – by this, I mean that if you get people on side by being kind, the likelihood is they will treat you with fairness but not with favour.

For my part, I have never once felt that my relationship with a journalist stopped me from being able to criticise the behaviour of their publication. I have on numerous occasions written for the *Sun* newspaper, which to many on the left of politics seems anathema (let's ignore that millions of working-class people read it, why don't we?). I did not write what they told me to write about, but about feminism and women's rights. I was even invited to a Christmas party at Rupert Murdoch's house one year, although it took me a while to realise this. The invite came in the post to my office, addressed to my husband and me, which is unusual for London events as my husband is not a political husband, preferring to feature on my Instagram in a three-stripe tracksuit painting Warhammer figures rather than by my side waving to the masses.* It said, 'To Jess and Tom', followed by the date and time of the function and an RSVP email with a name I didn't recognise, then signed off, 'Best wishes, Rupert and Jerry.' I rang Tom, confused, and asked, 'Do we know a gay couple called Rupert and Jerry? Because they have just invited us to their Christmas party.' Tom was as stumped as me. I only realised when I told the story to a colleague later that day and they suggested that it might be Rupert Murdoch and Jerry Hall. Honestly, people, I know you are super famous and powerful, but unless you are Madonna or Prince, I need a second name.

I really did not know what to do about this invitation. I was raised singing a song that I would not now encourage about throwing Rupert Murdoch on a bonfire.† I had heard all the terrible stories made public by the campaign group

---

* My husband is deeply political and very politically astute. His judgement, which I ignore at my peril, is better and more insightful than any high-level political advisor I have ever met. He understands people and cares deeply about politics but he does not feel the need to wear a badge and hates it if such a thing is demanded of him. He knows which badges he'd never wear, and he's picky about the ones he will. He wears one with my name on gladly. In case it is not clear, I love him very much; he is the cleverest, most competent human I have ever met, and I have met David Attenborough.

† 'Build a bonfire, build a bonfire, put the Tories on the top, put Murdoch in the middle and burn the blooming lot.' I am not proud of this, I hate this kind of imagery about killing politicians and political opponents now but it is a fact that I sang this as a child in the 1980s.

Hacked Off and campaigned alongside its victims. I gave evidence to the Leveson Inquiry about how terribly the newspapers represent women and their failures when reporting on domestic and sexual abuse. I wanted to be free to criticise this man's newspaper when I needed to. But I also really wanted to go and see his house. I asked my Bolshevik father and teacher of Murdoch bonfire song what he would do and he said that I should go just to see it. This was pretty much the reaction of everyone. 'Think of the anecdote,' said one friend.

On the evening of the party, I had to vote in Parliament so was only able to pop in for around forty minutes. I spoke to Rupert Murdoch for nearly a whole minute, in which time I told him that I was disappointed that his house didn't look like a bond villain's pad and just looked like a posh London flat. He looked at me nonplussed; he clearly had no idea who I was, nor did he care. In the remaining thirty-nine minutes, I discovered that very rich women party just like me and my girlfriends do; I watched as they fell about on a huge sofa drinking fizzy wine and cackling at in-jokes. What I had expected, I don't know, but I could have easily been around at my mate's houses in Birmingham. I took a photo of myself in the loo for posterity and I left. It was uneventful.

Since then, I have successfully criticised the actions of Murdoch himself; I have taken on the *Sun* and *The Times* (we shouldn't be so bloody snobby in the way we are so keen to criticise tabloids) when they got stuff wrong and I have also worked with the *Sun* on a series of successful campaigns to get better funding for women's refuges. The relationships we have with the media shouldn't always be characterised as on or off – they are far more complicated than that.

I need newspapers to back my campaigns; I especially need right-leaning Conservative-government-supporting newspapers to write stories about my campaigns, to research the topics that I care about and to get their readers to push the government to change stuff. The *Sun* newspaper is arguably Murdoch's biggest political UK mouthpiece. I abhor much of what he stands for and many of the things he has done (and also his house was nowhere near as exciting as I had hoped) but should I not seek to have a voice in his paper to win support for the most marginalised people in our society? The *Sun* has, for example, consistently backed my campaign to ensure that migrant women can access domestic abuse refuges just as easily as British-born victims can. This is more likely to get the government to give in than if the *Guardian* say it. I want and need both papers to say the same thing and pretending otherwise would simply be to put my needs before the needs of those women. Ministers are all too ready to roll their eyes at me when I present them with hard facts about how their policies are hurting vulnerable people; they say that I am shroud-waving or that I am leading with my heart, that they expect as much from me as a city-dwelling liberal. I need the help of the media to convince them that giving a shit about people is mainstream. It was pretty powerful when, in the domestic abuse committee, I could read an extract from the *Sun*. This is what I said to ministers that day:

This is not some liberal elite, *Guardian*-led campaign just for people like me, who might be expected to wave a banner. This week, the *Sun* newspaper backed the campaign to protect migrant women in this Bill. I am sure my father will be thrilled with this, but the *Sun* said: 'Jess Phillips is absolutely right. Domestic abusers don't discriminate, so why should the law discriminate against their victims?' I thank the *Sun* newspaper for its support.

When the *Sun* is awful to migrant communities, do I let them off? Absolutely not. I have and will continue to condemn any newspaper if I think they are lying or doing a disservice to migrants, women, victims – anyone who is shat on and marginalised. I criticise all newspapers in this regard, including the *Guardian*, who, for example, I felt overplayed the obituary of Peter Sutcliffe. I have torn strips off the BBC for trailing documentaries about famous domestic abusers without mentioning their victims, as if domestic homicide is a victimless crime. I have and will continue to try to work with all newspapers to cure them of their constant need to refer to men who kill their wives as 'loving fathers'. Every time the *Sun* or the *Mail* singles out Muslim communities unfairly, I will call them out. I wish I had the power to stop all this wrongdoing overnight, but I don't. But what I can do is work with journalists in Parliament, and they with me, knowing that we can very publicly and robustly hold each other to account.

This is not to say that I am never nervous and cautious of journalists; I absolutely am. When the phone numbers of certain journalists flash up on my phone screen, my immediate thought is, *Shit, what have I done?* Michael Crick and Brendan Carlin, both at the *Mail*, spring to mind. They are known for nailing politicians to the wall, both fairly and unfairly, or so many would argue. If you get a phone call on a Friday afternoon from a journalist or an unknown number, the dread that you have done something that will be the headline in the Sunday papers rushes over you like a cold shower. I am not sure why I fear this so much given how boring my life is, but I do. This can seem unfair, and feel like you are under attack, but it is their job, and surely the public wants journalists to be people who are willing to look in the cracks.

However, when looking in the cracks breaks the law or goes beyond the public interest – for example, delving into someone's completely irrelevant private life – then I think a line is crossed. And as we all know, this does happen, but in my own personal experience, while I have had to deal with journalists writing stories that were painful to me and people around me, I couldn't argue they were unfair.

Don't get me wrong, there are still a lot of problems with the way that different people are written about depending on the paper's allegiances. For some papers, breaking the ministerial code and quaffing champagne with Tory donors who then get a massive government contract is written up as if it is questionable but fundamentally not that bad. While in the same paper, if I were to so much as put in a 49p claim for paperclips that I then used at home rather than in my office, the headline would scream that I was a national threat to the taxpayer.

But at least I would get my say, too. One thing I didn't know before I became a person of interest to journalists is that there is a system in place with most mainstream newspapers and news outlets that ensures you are given a right of reply. In many cases, it is very hard for a journalist to publish a story accusing you of something if they have not informed you of it beforehand. If a big story is coming out in the papers, you will usually know about it the night before, so you are braced for it. Often in the right of reply politicians will just issue a denial or a 'no comment', but still, if a journalist hasn't sought this then they will struggle to have the story published. I discovered this during the sexual harassment in Westminster scandal when a lot of people seemed to push the stories coming out back to a better day by just hiding for a bit and putting their phone on silent. If you answer your phone, you are almost immediately done for, as a 'no comment' is usually considered enough to allow the story to run.

Many MPs will try to use lawyers to stop a story and, again, in my experience of the sexual harassment and abuse scandals, this works to a degree. If only we all had a team of highly paid lawyers on hand at any moment, eh? There is quite a lot a powerful person can do to manage how a story comes out – though not always, of course. Sometimes it all happens too fast and the competition between papers to get the first bite of the apple will see people tumbling onto the front pages. However, the scenes you see on television dramas, where the first the sleazy minister knows about a scandal getting out is when he sips his morning coffee in his dressing gown and picks up the paper, are pretty much entirely false. Politicians know what is coming and, to some degree, can limit the damage at least – although in many ways I think knowing that a story is coming is worse because of the horrible sense of foreboding.

The times when the press all gather outside a politician's home is something that I find very hard. I am no Jeremy Corbyn super fan, as you may know, but I think even I would have looked pretty grumpy if I had people camped outside my house every day asking me often inane questions. My husband would be apoplectic under these circumstances. There have been just three occasions when reporters or TV crews have turned up at my house, as living in Birmingham does give some protection from this. On these occasions, I politely said, 'Please don't film my house as it is a security threat to me and my children who also live here. I will call your producers and arrange a time I can speak.' This has so far always been met with gracious caution and an agreement not to put my house on the telly. My husband would have said, 'Get the fuck off my front drive' very forcefully had he been given the choice, but that would have been 'a story' and, while it does feel like an intrusion, these people are usually only trying to do their job. I am, after all, a public figure, and if you try to escape scrutiny it will chase after you all the harder.

It is one thing for me to have to be pragmatic about this – for one, I have had media training and understand the strategy for dealing with it – it is quite another thing when civilians have to deal with doorstepping by media because they or their family have made the news, often under very distressing circumstances.

I have to accept that, as much as I expect my privacy and family life to be respected, as long as it is fairly and respectfully done, I should also expect a certain degree of press scrutiny, even when it is uncomfortable. After all, I expect that of my opponents. But there are aspects of this scrutiny that are not equally distributed among all politicians. For example, if a woman is caught up in any kind of 'gotcha' story, it will be written up with at least ten times as many nods to her gender than a man would get, and with oddly dated descriptions, like 'racy', 'bossy', 'saucy', etc. It is so very 1970s.

The same goes for Black and Asian politicians who constantly have to battle much more intense scrutiny on the causes they take up, as if their loyalties to the country are somehow split. They also often have to put up with more attention focused on their personal lives, their relationships or parenting. This is all bullshit, without doubt, but the fundamental underlying issue is that as public representatives we must have people to broadcast our bullshit. I just wish they dealt it out more equally.

And the truth is that we need the journalists. If you have heard of the Windrush scandal, or you have seen an exposé on landlords in the UK charging young people sex for rent, or you are aware of the soaring number of children on free school meals, the reason you know this stuff is because good politicians and activists worked together with good journalists to tell you. They made sure that the stories of the victims of abuse and violence, the tales of Jamaican migrants wrongfully deported, the faces of the children of Grenfell Tower, were seen and heard and shared across the nation. I work alongside journalists who help me to shine a massive floodlight on issues I cannot get the government to act on. There is no campaign, no law I would seek to change, where I wouldn't be considering who my allies in the media are on this issue, or what the journalistic angle is. And this applies to the wider media, not just journalism: I have to think how I can get Lorraine Kelly, *This Morning* or *The One Show* to feature my story. I have to think about Brenda.

The media is one way of centring the voices of the people, not the politics. Rather than just hearing my voice demanding a change in the law to sentencing for domestic abuse, it should be the voice of the mother whose daughter died. It should be the families of the Grenfell Tower victims who feature in the videos about housing regulation. It should be words from the British citizens of the Windrush generation who faced unfair deportation that are heard decrying our immigration policies. It is always their stories that should be the heartbeat. When this happens, that is when journalism and politics are, together, an amazing force for good. And, of course, it works both ways: it isn't just me going to journalists and asking them to care about my issue and highlight it; editors also call me up and ask if I will champion the law change they and their readers are calling for in the aftermath of a year-long exposé their journalists have worked on.

The current system of reporting, like anything in politics, is at its greatest when it really, truly serves the people, rather than dishing up quick headlines, clickbait or easy political wins. There is much more of the former going on than you might think and everything that ever changed did so at least in part through this relationship. A campaigning journalist and a plucky MP is an absolutely winning bloody formula but often the public only sees us bickering on the telly, interrupting each other and always trying to get one up. Or they hear endless stories about our pay and our holidays and see mad headlines about royal boats and orgasms. The reality of what happens is far more inspiring; if only people knew.

11

A Rosette on a Donkey: Party Politics

'You could put a red rosette on a donkey and it would still win around here.'

You can replace the donkey with any animal of your choosing: I have heard this phrase where donkey has been substituted for cactus, pudding, steaming pile of shit, bag of skin and many others. People have, on many occasions, asserted to me that the only reason that I win my constituency in the general election is because my area will always vote Labour. This is palpably untrue; Birmingham Yardley was represented by the Liberal Democrats for a decade before I first stood and in my lifetime, it has pinned a red, yellow and blue rosette to the winning donkey.

Just for the sake of public record, a donkey, cactus or a sack (or any other receptacle) of excrement do not qualify under the electoral rules in our country. While our laws of universal suffrage may be better than elsewhere, they have yet to extend the vote to vegetable, mineral or non-human animals. You can of course dress up as any of these things and run for office, which is a time-honoured tradition in the British electoral system. It is one of the more amusing critiques of our party-political system. Some of my favourites over the years have included: a man dressed up as a fish finger, someone in an Elmo costume and, of course, that absolute classic, Count Binface and his previous incarnation Lord Buckethead. This noble character has, for a few years, stood in whichever constituency the current prime minister is running in. Thanks to this, he appears in a lot of the media coverage. There are few sights more sombre than the images of Theresa May when she lost her parliamentary majority by calling an unnecessary election which she thought would be a slam dunk. The pain and strain on our prime minister's face are evident as she faces the nation in this difficult and no doubt shameful moment from a sports hall in Maidenhead, stood next to a massive bloke with a huge bin on his head.

Count Binface is not a political candidate without policy, quite the opposite. His manifesto includes such gems as: bringing back Ceefax,* nationalising Adele (the singer), that any Czechs on the Irish border are allowed to stay there and, my personal favourite, all shops that play Christmas music before December to be closed down and turned into public libraries. Obviously, in addition to his national platform, Binface knew he had to appeal to locals in order to win his seat. In 2019, when standing against Boris Johnson in Uxbridge, his manifesto included vital local promises such as a pledge to move

---

* Younger readers may have to Google this. Back in the day, in a world before Google existed, Ceefax was how you booked a holiday or found out what was on the telly that evening. If you think this sounds deprived, you have clearly never experienced the hours of fun to be had playing the extremely slow-to-load game on Teletext called Bamboozle. So, really, you're the one missing out.

the hand dryer in the gents' toilet at the Crown and Treaty, Uxbridge, to a more sensible position.*

Yes, Binface is a joke candidate and that is the point, to be a figure of fun and take the piss out of the media circus that surrounds the elections of a high-level politician. There have always been political parties based on the idea that politics is a silliness and that there must be a 'none of the above' candidate on the ballot as an act of defiance. The Monster Raving Looney Party and their flamboyant leader Screaming Lord Sutch were the big players in this field when I was a kid. When I was a teenager, it was the Natural Law Party who took the crown. Founded in 1992, they were a political movement built on the principles of transcendental meditation, the laws of nature and their application to government. They had manifesto pledges about developing an individual's consciousness through the aforementioned meditation and bringing the individual and the country into tune with Natural Law so that unfavourable planetary influences would be neutralised. Sure, we can laugh now, but we never gave it a shot and look at the shitshow that is global politics today. Maybe we should have seriously considered cosmic yoga as a way to save the world; it is certainly no more ridiculous than Donald Trump telling people to drink bleach to cure coronavirus.

* The MP Stella Creasy and I once decided on a similar manifesto of minutia that we would instigate if we ever got to run the country as despotic dictators. She wanted to see an end to Coldplay, people who stop to look at their phone when walking in front of you on a busy street and those Beanie Baby teddies with the big eyes. I wanted to ban anyone who ever said 'Pacific' when they meant 'specific' and anyone who ever picked the minus amount of money to play for while appearing on ITV gameshow *The Chase*. We can laugh at Binface, but everyone has a list like this.

There have been many attempts to poke a hole in the very powerful two-party system in the UK, though never with much success. Even the Liberal Democrats, who have been in government, are basically a whisper of a political party nowadays. That's not to say that marginal parties or parties that lead on single issues can't rise to some power, influence and prominence. Look at how UKIP managed to scare the shit out of the two main political parties in the 2010s, causing the Labour Party to distribute mugs with the slogan 'Controls on immigration' and David Cameron to sign his political death warrant by pledging to have a referendum on Britain's place in the European Union. So scared was Cameron of a mutiny of backbenchers joining forces with UKIP, or that Conservative voters would defect in their hordes, that he literally changed the face of our country forever. All this, despite the fact that UKIP have only ever won a single seat in Parliament and that was only because a Conservative MP decided to desert to UKIP and hold a by-election in his constituency, where he was well known and well liked. Otherwise, they have never been able to get a single party member inside the palace. Maybe the political classes should have just said, 'Look, when enough people in the country care about this single issue enough to elect more than ten MPs, maybe, just maybe, we will then have a think about this single bloody issue.'

The Scottish National Party* are another example of a single issue turned into a successful powerbase. Their platform is essentially the single issue of Scottish independence but they have been so successful at positioning themselves as 'the third party' that they pretty much have a free rein to rule Scotland for the foreseeable. Many of the people who vote for them do not agree with Scottish independence; I have friends who have absolutely no interest in Scotland leaving the UK but who vote SNP because they are neither the Tories nor the Labour Party. 'None of the above' protest voting is the only way that any third party can rise to prominence in the UK, be it the SNP, the Liberal Democrats or UKIP.

This reliance on protest voting is also a manifestation of the politics of grievance as opposed to hope. Don't get me wrong, these political parties will all have manifestos that present a hopeful sun-soaked future, but there has to be an element in their campaigns, be it explicit or implicit, that is based on bashing the establishment, poking at people's grievances and essentially declaring the system broken. They need you to hate the two-party system in order to get your vote. In the 2010 elections, the Liberal Democrats did themselves some real damage by joining up with one of the players in that system. It was a betrayal to their supporters who thought

---

* The prime minister, or in fact any Tory minister, never fails to accidentally-on-purpose misremember the name of the Scottish National Party and with commendable discipline will always refer to them as the Scottish Nationalist Party (fair play, this is one of my favourite moves). The SNP hate this as they want to be seen as being all progressive and liberal, and obviously political nationalism has a nasty BNP and racist taste. They don't want to be called nationalists but that is what they are; I am not saying they are the racist type, as a rule, but they are nationalists, and I will never think of nationalism as anything but dangerous populism that breeds hatred and division.

that they had voted for 'none of the above', only to find that their votes had gone to one of the above regardless.*

Are people right to hate the party-political system? First, I must say most people don't hate it – most people don't give a toss one way or another about electoral makeup or electoral reform; they are too busy cracking on with their lives. The first-past-the-post versus a proportional system is a debate that truly excites the politically excitable and I have received hundreds of emails over the years from national campaigners and people determined that we change the electoral system. I can see why from a democratic point of view, however I can count on one hand the number of times electoral systems have been raised with me on the doorstep. I am not saying for a second that we shouldn't change our electoral voting system, but I am saying that it is not the nation's top priority.

What most people *do* want is for someone to give a shit about their neighbourhood, their jobs, their hospitals and their kids. So, does party politics deliver this? The case for the prosecution would say absolutely not unless you lived in a marginal seat or are lucky.

The rosette on a donkey quip has got an element of truth to it, in that in my years of frontline politics, I have seen how some safe seats on local councils and parliamentary constituencies can lead to really lazy light-touch represent-atives. I have seen how both Tory and Labour areas can

---

* One of my best friends who is a public sector worker voted Liberal Democrat in 2010 only to have her vote registered for the Tories – which is how she saw it. She felt genuine shame for the way she had voted and blamed herself for some of the actions that befell her profession and the lives of her deprived students as a result. The Liberals will struggle to bounce back from that.

become chiefdoms where the candidates are multiple members of the same extended family and political positions are treated as if they are social symbols to be given out rather than jobs that need doing. Being able to put 'Councillor' or 'the Honourable' in front of your name is, for some, the equivalent of having a flash car – or in medieval times, gloating about having gout. I have absolutely no idea why this is the case.

I am very proud to be an MP – heart-burstingly proud in fact, I am still chuffed when people ask me what I do for a living and I get to tell them. Yes, there is some status in it and obviously it is quite a rare job to have. And I am proud of how I got here, how I worked my way up the ranks from relatively humble start, took my home seat of Yardley from another political party and turned that marginal seat into a relatively safe Labour one through charm, hard work and a big wedge of luck. I did all that by the time I was thirty-three and the mom of two small kids living in a two-up, two-down. This is not everyone's route into politics. Boris Johnson, by comparison, grew up posh, went to a posh school, had a posh job and was elected to a safe Conservative seat in Henley, a place he had never lived and knew naff all about. He then packed it in to be Mayor of London and when he wanted back in, he got a plumb safe seat in Uxbridge – another place he didn't live or have any particular affiliation with.

I will never understand those in politics like Boris Johnson, and many others, who give up really quite affluent lives and far easier jobs to enter into politics. And yet some of the richest people in our country's history have hankered after the job of politician. Many Tory MPs have complained to me about the salary cut they took, often with the rider that they couldn't survive without their partner's salary. I can understand taking a hit like this if they had a calling on an issue like climate change or racial inequality, if they wanted to change the world and this was the job that could make that change happen. But I have absolutely no idea what Boris Johnson's calling is. Or David Cameron's, for that matter. What is it that they want for the world? Please feel free to pop your reasonable suggestions for an answer to this question on a postcard and send it in to 10 Downing Street, Westminster, London SW1A. I'm sure they would appreciate some ideas. For these people (and some exist in my party too, although it is admittedly rarer), I think it must just be the status of political office that they seek.

For me, becoming a politician was absolutely a calling. But it also changed my life, tripled my income and was a massively ambitious career move up. Some MPs, however, seem to be channelling more of a Veruca Salt in *Charlie and the Chocolate Factory* vibe: 'I want to be an MP! I want to be the mayor! I want to be a Lord of the Realm and sit on a throne of gold!' I cannot even say for sure that their motivations are *bad*; I just don't know what they are. This is not a Labour/ Tory divide; in the case of many Conservative MPs I know exactly what they stand for and why they are an MP, and for a fair few of them it was a real career step up. But there are also quite a few where simply being a Tory MP and being liked by whoever is the Tory leader seem to be the extent of their ambitions. These latter tend to stand in the safest Tory seats which offer them a comfortable job for life.

This is not to say that those safe seats are handed out immediately. Boris Johnson has not always had a clear run and he did stand in a no-hope safe Labour seat in Wales in the 1997 general election. This is not unusual; it seems as though all Tory candidates are expected to go through the motions of travelling around the country to stand in no-hope seats in Welsh mining towns or Glasgow ship-building communities before they are even considered for selection to a plumb safe seat.

On the face of it, it could appear there is something quite noble about this. Maybe there is something good about making politicians stand in seats they could never win, making them prove their commitment to the cause by being willing to lose for it. Right? Well, no. Not exactly. When I think about this flogging practice for new Tory candidates I am offended on behalf of the people in those seats. The candidates are not paying their dues to the residents of those places but to the Conservative Party. They are proving to a machine already oiled by privilege that they are willing to take one in for the team and that they can afford to do so. People like Boris Johnson and Jacob Rees Mogg carpet-bag around the country, using our democratic system to climb a ladder, without giving even the slightest damn about the people who live in those places. As if the people in poorer constituencies are toy soldiers to be swept aside in battle so that the colonel can rise up the ranks. It is actually grotesque.

This practice necessarily limits the kind of people who can take part. Jacob Rees Mogg may very well have been able to afford the three months of campaigning in the no-hope seat of Central Fife, hundreds and hundreds of miles from his home and his job, in order to go through the assault course set out by the Conservative Party for young hopefuls, but how could I ever have done that? Jacob Rees Mogg was twenty-seven when he went on his little political jolly to Scotland. He had family wealth and was a well-paid investment banker who could return immediately to that job. When I was twenty-seven, I had a newborn baby and a toddler, was working part-time at a charity offering care work and support to older adults and relied on the benefits system to top up my wages so that I could afford to go to work at all. Imagine if I had said to my boss and the older people I was caring for, 'I'm just going to pop to Scotland for three months to fight an election that I will definitely lose. I assume you are going to continue paying me and I will return to my job when it suits me. Thanks awfully, chaps. Don't forget that Mrs Blythe from Barn Lane needs taking to the shops on Wednesday and Alf is due to start at a new day centre next week. Take care, see you on the flipside of my political vanity.' I would have been sacked. *I* would sack me.

Don't get me wrong, I don't think that in order to be a good representative for an area you necessarily have to come from there. In every party, representatives will travel around the country standing in various seats, although I have to say this happens much less in the Labour Party than it used to and the electorate seem far more convinced by the local angle than before. I do, however, think there is a real problem with a party system where representatives are expected to put in their time standing in a place where they would never deign to live and, in return, these favoured sons (and occasionally daughters) are then gifted safe seats. Like a badge of honour for having mixed with the plebs. Maybe fewer seats would be safe seats, for any political party, if local candidates actually gave a toss about the local library facilities or schools.

Within this system, the no-hope-of-winning towns become the brown streets on a Monopoly board, the ones you pick up early in the game to tide you over until you can bag yourself Park Lane. But it is also crap for the Park Lane residents, too. Surely safe seats should not be given out like candy, by the HQs of political parties, to people who happen to be their pals – surely the most pressing concern should be who is going to be the best representative for the people in that area? All political parties would argue that it is the local party branch that chooses the candidates and this is of course true: local parties select from a list of people compiled by the regional or national arm of the political party, offering them a choice between favoured son A or favoured son B.

I don't want to give the impression that I wouldn't use whatever networks, power and influence I have to help someone who I thought would be a brilliant candidate try to win a seat. I have and I would again! I do this for people who are brilliant local campaigners or amazing national activists. Though I tend to only really do it for people who are not currently well represented in Parliament or on the local council: women, especially women of colour, people with disabilities and working-class people who give a toss about the community that they do actually live in.

The current system is often based on positioning and prioritising candidates who will be the best for the current leadership of a political party. In the Corbyn years of the Labour Party, when one of the real wedge issues between the factions of the party was the issue of how we select, reselect and deselect local candidates, the battle from the centre was never about better representatives and improved democracy as it purported to be; this was a smokescreen. It was always about getting rid of the people who didn't suit the leadership and bringing in people who did. Corbyn and his team parachuted people into seats – just as everyone else in the whole of political history has done.*

This party-political habit of handing out seats to some while the hopefuls pay their dues traipsing around the country is a curse on our system, in my view. At best, it provides political representatives who will be both good for the party and, by pure chance, good for the local area. At worst, it perpetuates a ruling class who travel all over our brilliant and varied nation and claim to know how those people need representing better than they do themselves, and ultimately delivers a snivelling loyal foot soldier to the party master. Red, blue, yellow, orange,† green – no matter the colour, candidacy in elections is a political party's greatest currency for power brokering within and they are all at it.

---

* I want to give a brief but necessary shout out here to Ed Miliband, under whose leadership this stuff no doubt went on but he did in my experience try to do something to find local people who were campaigning on the ground and encourage them to be candidates for their local regions. This is how I was found; the Labour Party targeted me to get involved in frontline politics after I won a series of local and national plaudits for helping my community through some scary and difficult times.

† It is a particular bugbear of my husband that the Liberal Democrats cannot settle consistently on a colour between orange and yellow. I can think of few better metaphors for the Liberal Democrats than this.

This would be the same no matter what electoral scheme we had; the parties would find a way to game the lists of candidates or the processes for selection. Personally, I think a preferable system would be an American-style primary election by the public, where the actual residents of an area vote for who they want to be their party candidate. In a Yardley context, this would mean anyone in the community could register as a Labour voter and would then be able to vote in the selection of the Labour candidate. It would be harder to game in one sense because it would broaden the pool of people with power; however, it would also make the race more geared towards those with the most money to spend on wooing the greatest number of people.

I would happily face this rigour and am fairly confident that I would win as my electorate are often more keen on me than my selectorate (the group of political party members who nominate the candidate). That said, I am not sure that British people really want to be in what seems in the US to be a near-constant election cycle. The US system does away with the need for a leader of the opposition and localising the candidate selection process rather than having it dictated from the top down means essentially starting from scratch with each election cycle. Famously, when asked about the 2017 general election, Brenda from Bristol (as you know, women called Brenda are always my political touchstones as they seem so delightfully no-nonsense) exclaimed, 'Not another one!' This general election followed the 2015 general election, the national referendum on the UK role in the European Union and, no doubt, some mayoral and local elections for Brenda. There just isn't the culture here for this kind of constant electioneering and people get tired of it. Also, as history shows us, the American system is by no means perfect. It is largely still beholden to the powers of the political parties and is certainly dammed by needing massive injections of cash from donors – we all know how well needing loads of money from powerful rich people can play out, especially when it comes to public trust in our representatives. On balance, I think I would rather party-political brokering than the brokering of the super-rich in our elections.

I do think that there is a need to look at the system, though. Politics remains brutally inaccessible to ordinary people and the fact that fewer than 2 per cent of the population join a political party shows us just how wedded to party politics the UK really is. I find it fundamentally unfair that there are constituencies in the UK with only a third of the population of my constituency and yet the two constituencies carry equal weight in elections, essentially making the votes of my individual constituents count for less. We could equalise the sizes of constituencies for fairness. We could follow a system like the election for the Scottish parliament, known as the additional member system. Each voter casts two votes. First, a vote for a candidate standing in their constituency (as we do in England); whoever gets the most votes in the constituency is elected using the first past the post method. The second vote is used to elect people from a 'party list' of candidates put forward by a political party and standing in a wider region made up of multiple constituencies. This vote is measured on proportional representation: the number of seats a party receives will roughly reflect its percentage of the vote. Under this system both local issues and proportional representation are considered.

We need to do something that makes this system fairer, better and more equal, but I doubt I will see it in my life-time because very few people actually give a toss which electoral system we use, they just want their bins collected on time. In general, present readership excused, people are far less worried than I am about who holds what power and where it is held, whether that be Westminster, Holyrood, the Senedd or in your local town hall. They just want a halfway decent public service and for politicians not to be feathering their own nests. I am afraid to say that people will not tolerate a long and exhaustive structural change until we have rebuilt trust in the political system and it is seen as a system that actually delivers for people. Without that trust, trying to change our electoral systems will just seem like self-indulgent political obsession.

12

Speaking Out or Showing Off?: When and Why MPs Rebel

I was raised in the Labour Party. I mean that literally. I went to Women's Liberation Playgroup preschool, which had been set up by a group of women from the Labour Party, including my mom, to ensure that women could work. Every event from my early memories – every gathering, bonfire night, celebration – was my family plus our Labour Party family. The Labour Party was like a religion in our house; it was the beating heart of every dinner conversation and every row, and every weekend activity was fitted around whatever party activity had to be done first. My childminder was a woman from the Labour Party, our vegetables were collected from the market as part of a Labour Party cooperative, my clothes were all handed down to me by people from the Labour Party, everything was about the Labour Party. I get that people feel passionate about their team, I really do. However, when I got to Westminster, I could not believe how much the institution of the political party stripped people of their gumption and drive. I saw it damn their dignity and, in the worst cases, I watched as political affiliations damned a person's morality.

The lesser of these two evils usually comes in the form of

an MP who, subject to the whim of the machine, will sign up to say and do pretty much anything that their bosses (or their bosses' foot soldiers, the whips) tell them to. Frequently, a new MP will stand in the Commons and read out a question that has clearly been given to them by a government whip in order to hand an easy pass to the prime minister or a Secretary of State at the despatch box. The question is designed to allow the Cabinet minister to say their rousing prepared line as if it were off the cuff and not a total set-up. In these instances, the opposition benches will all shout, 'Gis a job!', because this behaviour is associated with fresh MPs who, in their desperation to be noticed, are doing the bidding of their bosses, rather than their constituents. It is really embarrassing to watch an MP stand and, for example, ask of the Secretary of State for Health: 'Does the minister agree with me that this government has invested more than anyone else in our glorious NHS?' They literally read these out from scraps of paper, often with all the passionate delivery and broken intonation of an eleven-year-old kid reading Shakespeare aloud in class. It is cringeworthy, and it is not loyalty; it is desperation.

I don't know if this is a phenomenon of all governing parties. I assume it happened when Labour was in power but as I have only ever sat in the House of Commons in opposition it is something I only associate with Tory MPs. But we all do favours for our leadership teams: we all agree to speak in debates we aren't bothered about because our mates have asked us to come and row in, and we have all put in to ask departmental questions that our frontbench teams have asked us to. This is how the place runs. But to be so obviously sucking up to your boss in public is completely alien to me. If I were asked to do this, I would give a hard no.

The other painful experience for an MP is when their loyalty to their political party is strained by having to passionately defend a position they simply don't agree with, either in Parliament or on the TV. If I had a pound for every frank conversation I have had in the Westminster coffee queue with Conservative colleagues who disagree with what their party is saying or doing, I would never need to pay the 80p it costs for a cup of tea in there again. I have listened to Tory MPs exclaiming, 'What the fuck is he playing at?' or 'I know, I know, it is embarrassing,' who then have to somehow go and defend a position they think is crackers in the media.

We all do this to some extent, as you have to pick your battles. Everyone has a red line that they will not cross but when it comes to general bad performance by your party leader or a stupid policy or sentiment flouted by the Cabinet (or, I don't know, a senior advisor taking his car out for a spin as an eye test), you have to either avoid answering the question or you have to spin it. I am rubbish at the latter and usually end up in hot water because I will eventually give in to an interviewer and say, 'Yes, it wasn't the finest moment.' This is the everyday rub of party-political allegiances.

Perhaps you think you would never behave in this way, but if you allow yourself to be completely objective, it is likely that you would, and in fact, this is how most workplaces operate. Very few people steam into their boss's office to tell him or her what a dreadful job they are doing this week or feel that, on a point of principle, they must publicly slag off anyone in their team who is doing a crappy job. For the most part, you do the best you can in your own job and you keep your head down; it is essentially the same for MPs, with the difference that we have TV cameras in our faces. But it is not these minor violations forced onto us by party loyalty that I want to talk about. These are absolute peanuts compared to what I witnessed when I started supporting people in Westminster who had been sexually harassed, abused or even raped by senior members of all the major political parties. This went far beyond the uninspiring and into the actually pretty frightening.

I saw political friendships, alliances and party-political brands given more weight than morality on many occasions. You would think that, as someone who had spent years working with victims of domestic and sexual violence, I might have become acclimatised to the brutal realities. You might think I was used to many people turning a blind eye to perpetrators of abuse when they are people that they know and love or respect. You could assume I was fully aware that the perpetrators in such cases are manipulative, often with the skills to get away with their behaviour and exploit a position in society that is usually more powerful than the people that they abuse. And of course I *was* aware of all this. But it still shocked me. Westminster was the place I had aspired to be, a place I wanted entry to because it was here that we could change the world for the better. I found terrible disappointment.

I'm going to stop here for a moment to deliver a short lecture on this subject. You may have come here for titbits on Westminster or to get an insight into what it is we MPs actually do all day and I hope I have been able to offer both, but I'd like to grab just a minute here to impart some hard lessons. I will pretty much dedicate the rest of my career to trying to get people to understand this, and so it would be churlish to miss this chance. Here we go. People who you know, like and respect are perpetrators of domestic and sexual abuse. That's it. You'd be surprised how hard many people find this to swallow. Over the past decade, and with huge thanks to the #MeToo movement, the average citizen has come to realise that everyone knows a victim of abuse. From being a crime that was hidden away, considered to be the stuff of gruesome films set in the north of England, abuse and harassment towards women has emerged into the public consciousness, becoming more widely talked about and, hopefully, more widely recognised as a result. We are now all pretty good at accepting that if we know a woman, we know a woman who has been groped, and most of us could tell a story about someone we know who was in a 'nasty relationship'. We have started educating ourselves to see controlling behaviours much more clearly and to recognise the many forms that this can take; we are far better at understanding that domestic abuse is a many-headed beast and that we know people who have suffered it in its various forms. This is real progress. Pat yourselves on the back; the regular experience of womanhood is being recognised.

However, while we were taking a step forward in this respect, we have somehow managed to enter into a state of thinking about perpetrators of domestic abuse as monsters from a fairy tale, assuming that they are the friends and family of other people – not anyone we know. Statistically speaking, if everyone knows someone who has been groped, then everyone knows a groper. To dismiss this fact you would have to believe that there are just one hundred terrible men roaming the country abusing all the women. We all know this isn't the case. It is far harder to accept that you know, like and, in many cases, love a man who has abused or is abusing a woman in some way – but it is almost certain that you do. I do. I know and like lots of men who have behaved more than questionably with women in their past. I don't ignore that fact and when I hear tales of sleeping with prostitutes abroad, I make clear to those people that I am disgusted and that it is a form of sexual exploitation and I consider them to be an abuser. When I hear stories about encounters with drunken women shared around like candy in a pub (this has admittedly waned as I have got older), I tell them that it sounds like they are talking about raping women. Women have told me stories about men I know who have hit them and controlled them, harassed them and harmed them.

I can already feel the critique and the violent Twitter response, decrying me for saying 'all men are rapists'. I am absolutely not saying that. I am married to a man and I hope we are raising two men who consider women to be their financial, social and sexual equals. Most of the men I know are good and have no need to be lectured on this subject – but I also know men that do. I don't need to be absolutist or to hate them and try to ruin their lives, but I do have to speak up when they are arseholes and I do have to trust and believe women who tell me about abusive behaviour even if I am friends or acquaintances with the perpetrator. I can even like them afterwards, but if I ignore *her* because I like *him* then the problem will never, ever go away. Pretty much every perpetrator of violence against women has mates and people who love him.

As a society, we will never be able to get over the epidemic of violence against women and girls unless we face up to the fact that we all know perpetrators. They grew up with us. They look and sound like us. They drink fancy coffees and eat sourdough toast. They are people who love their grand-children and put a quid in a jar for them each week so they can save up and buy them that good Lego set. They volunteer to do youth tennis coaching with kids from the local estate. They work in your kid's primary school. These examples are all from cases I have handled directly, cases where the men have been convicted of violence, abuse and coercion. Yes, convicted, not just accused. And the convicted are just the tip of the iceberg.

When a spotlight was shone on my workplace, into the long, winding labyrinth of the Palace of Westminster, there were some bad men lurking. There were many more *not* bad men, but the story about the MP who didn't grope an underling is less newsworthy. And, unfortunately, if your workplace had a staff of 100 journalists working there all the time and the world's media investigating it, it would find the same proportion of people behaving poorly.

When I began supporting victims within Westminster, I found that the thinking I have outlined above was writ large in most of the powerful places I turned to for help. People were more than willing to believe misdemeanours by their political opponents but they were far less likely to believe accusations levelled against people that they liked, let alone do something about these accusations. Really good people, who you knew cared about these issues, would suddenly say, 'Surely not him, he's such a nice bloke.' People told me that

I was exaggerating or insisted that while 'something' might have gone on, they had heard from him and, 'Believe me, there is much more to the story than meets the eye.'

On one occasion, I had seen reams of text messages from the perpetrator apologising for their behaviour and admitting to stepping over the line, as well as a message threatening to have people sacked. However I was told by a colleague that I shouldn't look any further into the baseless accusations in the newspapers because the bloke in question had explained to them that the woman was just on the warpath as she had been bad at her job and was after attention. It is amazing how quickly people are willing to believe the word of their mate; they can't help it. It's also a way to feel protected from harm as it is reassuring to believe that these actions are something that other people do, not people in your immediate circle.

Those victims, both male and female, who come forward publicly and speak about their experiences in the press, have always faced accusations of being an attention seeker. They are immediately reminded by loads of people who want to ignore the problem that it is the courts and employment laws that should deal with that (and obviously this system is doing a flawless job) – it is not the job of the press. The argument for the defence that going to the media discredits a person's testimony is utter bullshit. Because, in my long and extensive experience, every single victim who came forward to the Conservative Party, to the Labour Party, to the Liberals and the SNP, was totally ignored and sidelined until there was a sniff of press attention, when all of a sudden the political parties had to prove they were doing something.

In every political party, I have watched people delight in

the disgraces of other parties while kicking their own cases into the long grass. I watched Conservative MPs who hated John Bercow suddenly become very vocal about trying to clean up bullying and harassment rules just to be able to stick the knife into him. And yet the very same people had said nothing when there were complaints about their mates like good old Damian Green. One backbencher, James Duddridge, who had been trying to get rid of the Speaker for ages on various grounds, delightfully alighted on the bullying scandal as a new weapon to attack an old foe. He approached me in Portcullis House when I was eating my lunch and asked me to sign a motion about bullying by the Speaker because he knew I was helping to advocate on this issue. I told him that since he had never once given a toss about bullying in the past, since he had never made any effort to help victims of bullying in the workplace in all the time I had spoken out against it, since I had never seen him or spoken to him at any event highlighting these issues, no, I wouldn't be signing. I said I would sign it when he would sign one for all of his colleagues that I had disclosures about.* There were a lot of people who, like Duddridge, suddenly cared about this issue; I don't believe they gave even one shit about the alleged victims who were likely mere chess pieces in their power games.

It was not just the Conservatives who did this, the Labour Party excelled in it at the time. On one occasion, I

---

* I supported the people who came forward in the case of John Bercow and called for historic cases to be heard against him, and I still think that this should be the case. I like John Bercow but I think he should face the exact same rigour of an improved system of disclosure, investigation and sanction as the people I don't like.

rang Labour headquarters, probably for the third time that fortnight, with another complaint that had come to me. I expressed very clearly to the member of staff that the victim did not want this to be public and wanted to know whether if she put in a complaint the person would be suspended, thus causing a media spotlight. In this instance, we are talking about harassment at work rather than any physical or sexual abuse. The answer I got back, which was disgusting but was at least honest, was, 'You and I both know, Jess, it depends who it is.' Had it been a friend of Jeremy Corbyn, the answer would have been 'No, they won't be suspended'; had it been someone from another faction, then the answer would be yes.

I watched the Labour Party crow about Damian Green and Michael Fallon's resignations from the Cabinet while picking apart and endlessly delaying the cases in their own ranks. I watched them largely resist the changes called for by women who came forward with stories of people being raped and assaulted. I watched them profess feminism, but only for the women that they liked. On one occasion, I was directly asked to 'have a word' with a victim who had come forward to me and ask if he really wanted to go ahead with the complaint because the person he had made complaints against wasn't well and it might not be fair on them. This fell on completely factional lines and was really about people high up in the Labour Party trying to protect their own. They were happy to have this new tool to use against opponents but had no intention of employing it against their allies.

When I demanded suspensions, changes to rules and

regulations to protect the staff and volunteers working in politics, the argument constantly returned to me was that we had to be really careful about reputational damage. I have long suspected that the reason our rape conviction rates are so poor, the reason that domestic abuse deterrence is weak and rarely works, is because we live in a society with a justice system largely designed and created from a male perspective. Most people still think it would be worse to be accused of rape than to be raped; it is more shocking to say someone is a child abuser than for a child to be abused. We need *at the very least* to equalise these ideas in our head. I was constantly told by high-ups from every party that reputation came before my concerns about safeguarding. The fact that we leave staff and constituents at the hands of an accused abuser who retains their position of power and influence seemed to just be met with a shrug. I asked people with power if they would be happy if their child's school had such an attitude towards safeguarding. I was told 'it's not the same'.

While all this was going on, I would often walk through the tearoom at work and see Charlie Elphicke, a man facing a police investigation for sexual crimes, being quite clearly lovingly supported by his colleagues. On two separate occasions, I appealed to the Conservative Chief Whip, asking him to consider how it looked to victims when they saw Charlie Elphicke given back his position in the party so that he could help provide the numbers the Tories needed on certain votes. All this under the premiership of a woman who famously wore a t-shirt that said, 'This is what a feminist looks like'. It isn't. The Chief Whip weakly told me that there was nothing he could do.* That Charlie had not been charged with anything.

Charlie Elphicke, meanwhile, went around convincing everyone that he was the one who had been wronged by an unfair process. People kept repeating the same line to me, 'The poor man, he doesn't even know what the charges against him are, he hasn't heard from the police.' He had found a groove that worked with our colleagues and boy did he run with it. It worked because his friends and contemporaries could imagine how distressing it would be for them in his shoes, accused and waiting for months while the police investigated. They never tried to imagine themselves as junior members of staff, scared for their jobs unless they let their boss touch them up. Most were not familiar with how long these cases take – this case was not unusual. Maybe they haven't done much victim support, but from sexual offence to court within a year would be a lucky break.

But Elphicke had his narrative of unfairness to spread around Westminster and it worked; he even, and this takes some balls, tried it on me. Not to my face, you understand – he is essentially a very weak figure of a man when up against someone who is at least his equal and he would struggle to come close to my ability to defend a position on anything, let alone this. He would certainly have been frightened of confronting me in person: I don't have a quiet voice and

* I want to give a shout-out to Anne Milton, the Deputy Chief Whip at the time when the Elphicke complaint came in, who believed the women, acted properly, supported them and then gave evidence at his trial. She is an exemplar of decency and that is why, in the end, the Tories kicked her out – because she wouldn't toe the line.

people would have heard. Instead, he did the Westminsteriest thing: he sent me a personal note. I still have it, kept for posterity. Written on a small A5 piece of notepaper with the green Portcullis symbol embossed at the top and headed with 'Charlie Elphicke MP', the note reads:

> Dear Jess
>
> Just a short note to let you know that I saw your tweet yesterday. I want to make it clear that the shocking and awful accusation made against me by the Sunday Times has never been put to me by the Police or anyone. And when I asked the ST for details, they would not tell me.
>
> So, I am writing to say this is a dreadful accusation. It has been levelled in such a way I cannot make answer – except to say I would never do something awful like this. I would never hurt anyone.
>
> The past six months has been awful for me and my family. We must take care not to confuse accusation with evidence or allegation with proof. Nor to allow trial by media, that is the job of the Courts of Law. To do otherwise causes great damage to our justice system and the rule of law and has cost lives too. Not for publication – just a personal note to you.
>
> Best wishes
> Charlie

On 30 July 2020, Elphicke was found guilty on three counts of sexual assault. On 15 September 2020, Elphicke was given a sentence of two years in prison.

It's always good to be patronised and lectured on the rule of law and what causes harm by a sex offender. I don't doubt that he still believes he is right and I am wrong in this. He could easily have been found not guilty, as these cases are incredibly hard to prosecute. Had he been found not guilty, or had the investigations been dropped, everyone would now be accusing me of causing harm for simply seeking that these cases be properly investigated. For me, the safeguards put in place to ensure that the people whose lives are entrusted to senior political figures are the priority and this matters more to me than reputation.

Charlie wasn't alone in peddling this shtick. I have heard, again and again, the complaint of 'unfair accusations' being spread around by politicians trying to protect their reputations and their friends. I wish they would realise that, in trying to cover this stuff up for the sake of 'the party', half the time they will definitely get away with it, sure, but the times they don't will make them look even worse and will make people hate not just their political party but all politics and politicians, too. This behaviour makes the public think we are all sleazy gropers pressuring our personal assistants to give us massages. Yuck!*

Political affiliations and protecting your brand or your

---

* After years of work by victims, the unions and cross-party MPs who fought pretty hard, there is now an independent complaints system in Parliament which I believe to be free of political influence. The Labour Party has improved its complaints system to have an element of independence and I continue to work with campaigners and members to make the Labour Party system the best, fairest and safest it can be. This is a work in progress that demands that protectionism comes second to safety and I think we will get there. The Conservatives, as best I know, have done very little to improve their internal processes and feel free to read about the goings on in the SNP in the case of Alex Salmond. It will get better but, in the process, people like me will be accused of ruining more lives than the perpetrators. Don't worry, I'm used to it.

faction at any cost is without doubt behind the very worst ravages of party politics I have witnessed. The Labour Party was my church, my school and my family when I was growing up but I can be critical and honest with them without being considered a disloyal sinner. I would give my right arm and my left leg for these political powerhouses to realise that if they were more upfront in dealing with criticism, more honest when stuff went wrong, then the chances are that their stock would rise. We still live in a political system under which showing any sign of contrition, or admitting a mistake rather than spinning it to look like something you intended, is a sign of weakness. The truth is quite the opposite: learning from your mistakes and owning them is a sign of strength and it takes real courage to do it, far more so than this bullshit male gaze idea of strength and brilliance that never cocks up.

Loyalty, patronage and the desire to keep power where it currently resides are my main criticisms of a party-political system that I think is largely flawed but which, like democracy itself, is the best system available. Loyalty to the party can do very strange and corrupting things to people, as well we know from the history of the twentieth century. People with power often know when they are doing something wrong, but they do it nonetheless on the behest of their political party or leader.

In the world of Westminster politics, loyalty is mocked, not necessarily unfairly, as self-interest in most cases. Slights against junior ministers are made when they go along with the party whip in a vote that you know they feel uncomfortable with and it is always presented as them wanting to keep their job. There is no doubt that there is often some truth in this but it would be entirely unfair to categorise all loyalty to a party line as simple self-preservation. Sometimes it is a case of trying to preserve good work that you have done or are in the process of doing in your department; if you resign on principle there is always the chance that some zealot will be put in your place and the project you were about to deliver on legal aid or new bus fleets in rural England might not get through. There are two ministers I know, both barristers,* held in high regard by the legal profession, who were distraught by the UK government's actions in 2020, when, as part of the UK's withdrawal from Europe, they passed the Internal Market Bill, which broke international law – though only, according to the Secretary of State for Northern Ireland, in a 'specific and limited way'. So that's okay then. They did not hide their feelings in the tearoom, they bled them all over the floor. When I retorted, 'Well, resign then, make a stand,' they responded simply and sadly that their jobs would just be given to people who would be even worse. There is an element of occupying a space at times, which some may call cowardice, but at least it is a loyalty to a project and to the people of the UK, rather than loyalty to a party logo.

And then there is party disloyalty and the many and varied reasons behind that. When you act against your party whip on principle, people will herald you as being bold and brave.

---

* Who isn't a goddamn barrister in Parliament? Barristers are ten a penny, hands down the most common profession, yet somehow, they still manage to maintain some kind superiority and air of the unusual. When Keir Starmer became the leader of the Labour Party there were all sorts of articles written about who in Parliament is the most eminent lawyer, like *Total Wipeout* for lawyers. I am sure children in playgrounds across the country are saying, 'My dad's a more eminent lawyer than yours'. It gets a bit snobby.

There are famous examples of this, such as Labour MP Robin Cook resigning from the Cabinet over the Iraq war, putting the concerns of the people of the UK and for the people of Iraq and his sense of what was right before his position or his party. Tory MP Tracey Crouch belongs in this category too. Tracey resigned from a ministerial post because the government refused to enact a policy that would have curtailed the use of gambling machines for those who struggle with gambling addictions and the horrors that ensue from that. She resigned to make the government listen to her, to express the seriousness of her concern on the issue and she won. The policy she had fought for was enacted. These are noble breaches of loyalty, where loyalty to the country and its people overrides loyalty to the party. This is the way it should always be. My loyalties go: constituency, country, party, in that order.*

Having said that there are opportunities for noble, kind and good disloyalty, never assume that such actions are motivated by principle and sheer righteousness. Always try to look for what the outcome of an act of political dissent is about: if it doesn't change anything for the people it aims to serve but just causes a massive media hoo-ha where that politician ends up heralded as the purest of the pure, then I would take it with a massive pinch of salt.

Let's take a look at a number of reasons for party disloyalty

* Obviously in real life, my family have my first and most strident loyalty and if my politics was hurting them and they asked me to stop I would. It does and has hurt them in the past, they live under a constant security threat and unwelcome intrusion into our private lives, but they have never asked me to stop because they don't think it would be a solution to the problem.

that I have seen in my political career. Some are more reasonable than others:

1. Because of loyalty to your constituency. This is a
   biggy and is usually about specific issues that might
   affect your constituents, such as legislation on
   new high-speed rail lines that will smash through
   your constituency and displace 400 people. Fair
   enough if you decide to break the party line on
   this. Constituency issues are usually considered an
   honest and understandable objection. It is important to say, however, that we are *representatives* of
   our constituents and our local party members; we
   are not delegates. There is a huge and important
   difference. A delegate takes forward an agreed and
   mandated position from the group and abides to
   vote accordingly, regardless of personal opinion. A
   representative is there to listen to and work with the
   people and represent their lives but is not mandated
   to vote a certain way. For example, if all my constituents were anti-abortion or pro the death penalty
   (they are absolutely not), I would still never vote
   for those things. They would, of course, have every
   right to ditch me for a representative who loved
   these positions; that's the gig.
2. To change the position of your party or your country. Before your party decides its position on a
   matter, there will be a lot of discussion between different teams and whips. If enough of you think the
   party needs a nudge in a different direction then the

threat of this bloc not voting with the party might shift its position. This is all part of the jockeying that goes on before votes on big issues of the day and is quite normal. It is how specific groupings or factions in political parties can hold a balance of power. If truth be told, in most political parties, zealots and ideologues are much better at flexing this muscle than progressives because they are usually more willing to tear things down. And although the sensible, reasoned voices far outweigh the aggrieved zealots in all political parties, they don't group together as well, and when they do, they tend to try to form compromises rather than laying down ultimatums. I am sad to say this often means that the loudest, angriest voices do a better job of changing party positions and this is how we have become so very polarised over the past decade.

3. Rebelling for rebelling sake. This is just plain old showing off. To put things in context, even in the five years of Jeremy Corbyn's leadership, when I found his tactics to be utterly abhorrent, at times offensive and sometimes actually dangerous for me, rarely did I not vote with the whip in Parliament. On one occasion, over the Migration Bill, when the Labour Party for some weird reason was not going to vote against what was a horrific and unworkable suggestion, I said publicly that I was going to defy the whip and so did many others and we were listened to at the last minute. Other than that, I broke the whip twice: once on a vote on child poverty

and another on a vote about keeping the UK in the European Single Market.* But people will also rebel in this way not to try to improve the position of the party, or even because it will make any difference to the people they claim to be fighting for, but because it makes them look good and it keeps alive an internal political grievance of their tribe. It is very tedious, it is very selfish and it repeatedly hands their opponents a win, while further damning the vulnerable group they claim to be defending. Call me a cynic, but I bet you a million pounds that if these people were kicked out of their party if they did this more than three times, they would suddenly find themselves a lot less righteous after two infractions.

4. Gang warfare. This sort of disloyalty is to spite the party for not favouring their group enough, for not making them feel like the biggest, best, most powerful politicians in the park. You see it a lot: a load of politicians from a particular gang indulge in a very public stropping off against their party whip. If you

---

* On this last one, I voted against the party whip for a rare reason in politics: because I sat through the debate on the single market and I actually let what people were saying convince me one way or another. This is not usual; the debate that precedes a vote rarely has a bearing on the outcome of the votes cast. But on this occasion, I was listening to the debate and a comment by Charlie Elphicke was so offensive to me that I felt I had to vote against whatever the position was he was taking. He basically tried to tell people like me that we have no idea about the effect of migration on an area. I come from Birmingham, where I barely know a single family where at least one person isn't a first- or second-generation migrant, and here was this man telling me I could never understand what living with freedom of movement was like. What a twat! I could not vote in the same lobby as him after that. The Labour whip under Corbyn told me I should. I didn't.

were to ask any one of the people involved about the detail of their objection to the policy, they would almost certainly draw a complete blank. The best example of this was the leaked WhatsApp conversation of the European Research Group (ERG) where Nadine Dorries, strident Brexiteer, didn't understand the basics of being in a customs union and asked her colleagues what it was all about. This was a woman who believed so staunchly that we should leave the customs union that she was calling for the resignation of members of her own government for supporting it. She didn't seem to know what she was fighting for at all, she was just fighting, her gang against another.

Having spoken at length about the ravages that loyalty can bring, I am now going to launch a full-scale defence of it. We must be careful, as consumers of political debate and drama, of mistaking loyalty to the party whip as indifference to the issue or as party deference. Without a party line, without a consensus, without a group of people sticking together, politics would be an absolute car crash. If MPs all moved entirely as individuals, guided only by their own personal principles rather than an agreed set of party principles that are then voted on by the people, literally nothing would ever get done. We would have 650 micromanagers shouting about every parochial thing that would secure their power.

Loyalty and discipline and agreeing to a grown-up compromise is likely to lead to better, stronger and more appealing governance that is in the long run better for the people. I will never get everything that I want, often I am disappointed with the lukewarmness of a position, but I am part of a team that has to work together.

My loyalty to the Labour Party doesn't blind me to its faults, it makes me want to work with others to keep it thriving and progressing. Collective responsibility that binds representatives to the position of their leadership and their party is the only way that the system can work. Dissent is fine, it keeps all sides in check and strength-tests policy and position. It also ensures a big-picture view of politics; I would never want to be in Parliament only ploughing my own furrow and the furrow of my constituents. I also care about where you live, even if it's nothing like where I live. I also care about the rest of the world. My political party enables me to be part of an organisation that operates on all these levels and allows me to have a foot in all these camps and a chance at making them work. The price for that is that I act loyally to my party and back it up in its movements. Not blindly, loyally.

Loyalty matters: it matters in your workplace, it matters in your family. It makes a group of people into a cohesive machine that can move together. Party politics matters to me and I will defend it while trying to bend it into a better, fairer shape. But this is not just a matter of loyalty. The reason I will passionately defend the party politics I grew up with is because it can be very beautiful.

You might not be surprised to hear that I am going to base the argument for this on a woman called Brenda – not an imagined Brenda but a real woman I know. Brenda is a member of the Labour Party in my constituency who joined in support of Jeremy Corbyn. Although she has been a left-leaning voter all her life, it was Corbyn who made her rejoin after many years. Brenda is in her sixties, she is not originally from Birmingham but from down south, she goes to church and is part of other political movements such as the campaign for nuclear disarmament. Brenda is possibly my favourite person in the world – certainly my favourite beyond those I am bound by blood or legal contract to favour above others. Brenda has absolutely no side on her, she doesn't take herself too seriously, she loves a joke at her own expense, she cares deeply about the people in our neighbourhood and she cannot believe the bloody cruelty of the government at times (although when she says this she apologises for swearing). Brenda loved Jeremy Corbyn and she knew very well that I didn't; we joked about it often. Setting our differences aside, Brenda turns up at my office day in day out to stuff envelopes, deliver leaflets and count endless literature into piles. She always brings biscuits and can't believe it when I send her a Christmas card because I am a fancy MP. Brenda is never trying to do anything but be a service to a politics that she believes can bring about a better society.

Political parties are not perfect and party members will bitch and moan about their own party far more than any other. But political parties give people a place to join with other folks to try to improve the whole neighbourhood, the whole region, the whole country and the whole world. Brenda just wants a place where she can be useful in trying to make things a bit better for people. And the Brendas of the world are worth all the skulduggery of powerful actors and those who build greasy poles for others to climb up. Brenda and I would almost certainly never have crossed paths had we not been thrown together on a cold windy night, both wrapped up in scarves, bobble hats pulled on tight, ready to go and ask people in Yardley what they wanted and needed. Only religion, political conviction, patriotism and, possibly, football would make people stand in the cold like this, united in purpose and filled with hope.

Without political parties, how would this manifest? In the feminist movement or the LGBT+ rights movement, for example. I often see people come together to fight on single issues, seeking improvement step by step. Of course, this would be hard to do without some of those actors holding political power, and without a political vehicle movements such as these would be more single issue. I would also argue these movements could become far more skewed by grievance rather than possibility, although this is undoubtedly a feature of all opposition politics and, frankly, I think this will continue to be the case until politics steps up the optimism over criticism.

People need a magnetic north to guide their passions and hopes into a coherent plan, and party politics can provide this. I am not for one second saying that I haven't been in Labour Party meetings that felt like the place where good ideas and hope go to die. I have been in meetings where people have raised grievances with the party from 1974, some seven years before I was born. They are absolutely full of tedious, pain-in-the-arse moments and attract many pain-in-the-arse people. But for every person who wants to talk for two hours over clause 7.2 of the code of conduct for members there is a Brenda who just wants her grandkids to have a fairer crack at things than she did and is willing to show up to make it happen.

For every meeting-hogging ideologue, there is a brilliant activist who wants to get on with the job. I will now shamelessly steal a story from my excellent colleague Rachel Reeves, as it gives a perfect illustration of this. Rachel was guest speaker at a local Labour Party event in Teesside in the north of England. She had delivered her fifteen-minute speech and was wrapping up the forty-five minutes of Q&A with the audience. Rachel had fielded questions about everything from Brexit to socialism to the north–south divide. The session was running over, as always, and the local party chair was just bringing proceedings to a close when someone shouted from the audience, 'Rachel, is it now time for class war?!' Before Rachel could even begin to answer, the brilliant and probably battle-weary party secretary, primed from many a meeting with this particular gentleman, simply replied, 'No, Alan, now it's time for the raffle.'

I believe in political parties as a vehicle to organise people in a local area to do good, not just to seek power. In my constituency, we try to help, we raise money, we do regular food drives. Some members of my local party volunteer hours of their time to attend disability benefit tribunals with my constituents so they don't have to face it alone. I have members who run surgeries from my office helping people with all sorts of things. Yes, we do all that campaigning stuff and whinging at each other and our opponents, but there is something about intrinsically knowing that we are on the same side that helps us get things done.

The political party system in Westminster is of similar

value: it helps me know where I stand and provides me with a solid base, and it enables a wide pool of knowledge and expertise. If I had to have an opinion on absolutely everything, without the support of someone who knows far more than me on the subject, I would be absolutely buggered. How Caroline Lucas, the solitary Green MP, copes without a squad I simply do not know; she must have amazing staff.

Similarly, the party-political groups in Westminster offer a genuine camaraderie in a job that is often long and thankless. There are all sorts of people and groups that I lean on; one of the strongest is the year you were elected. I am class of 2015 and find a huge amount of comfort and solidarity with other members of this group. My cohort currently leads the Labour Party, which is nice. We look out for each other, we organise events for each other and we amplify each other's voices. When votes are needed for committee places or other obscure parliamentary bodies, you can usually expect a block vote from this group of people in your favour. Even the people I might not naturally like or politically align get at least one tick for being in my cohort. Undoubtedly what keeps us together, stronger than anything else, is the memory of Harry Harpham, the MP for Sheffield Brightside, who died of cancer only a year after we were elected, and, of course, Jo Cox. The day before Jo Cox was murdered, the intake of 2015 had all been to her house to have a party. That night, we gave out silly awards to each other and raised our glasses to the memory of Harry, who could no longer be with us. Jo was murdered thirty-six hours later. These shared events are bound to build bonds that are hard to break and form a protective feeling towards each other that can at times seem unreasonable or biased but that has at its heart camaraderie and loyalty.

I have friendships across the aisle with Conservative colleagues that I value deeply. There are many with whom I have a really good laugh and can happily share a cup of tea or a pint with. There are a few who I know I could turn to if I needed them. But when the chips are down, these people are from a different team and that's who they have to back. No harm, no foul, that's the way it goes; they wouldn't harm me, but they are often limited in how they could help me.

Political parties are not perfect, far from it, but I just cannot come up with another way we could make the system work. I am certain that reform is needed in every party in the land and I also know that while the public would like us to disagree, they would like us to do so more agreeably, and they would like us to work together on the stuff we can agree on. There will always be willy waving and one-upmanship (and I choose these terms entirely deliberately) in the two-party system. Pluralism and coalitions might one day work, as they do elsewhere, but I just cannot imagine it because here smaller parties are too often reliant on the politics of grievance and protest voting.

I am afraid that the mainstream parties have fallen into this trap, too. Of late, political parties have relied on what people hate, or can be convinced to hate, as the unifying factor, rather than good governance and hope for the future. The more this happens, the more our country moves away from decent, consensual democracy. Slagging off all institutions, the press, the courts, the immigrants, 'the others' – it's all pretty destabilising. Unless we get back to a decent trusted party system where, ideological differences aside, people govern according to their idea of the common good rather than in order to grab more power and Facebook follows, then we should expect to see people storming our political buildings dressed like a bull. Don't judge party politics by bad political parties.

Conclusion

Why We Need Politics

When I was twenty-two, I found out I was pregnant with my first baby. It was a surprise, which is a nice way of saying that it was a mistake – a mistake I have gone on to feel was a blessing (albeit a knackering one). As a young person starting out in the world, I was fairly transient and, in the previous five years, had lived in around ten different addresses. I was working as an office administrator in the day and in pubs on the evenings and weekends. I had quite a lot of debt from my years at university and, just like most people aged twenty-two, had little in the way of long-term plans or security.

The baby in my belly changed everything overnight. I needed roots. I needed to stay living somewhere for more than six months and I needed to find a way to both earn money and look after this baby. I wasn't on my own; I had the man who is now my lovely husband by my side. He had at the time only been my boyfriend for a few months but he seemed unfazed. He too lived transiently in house shares with little security but he had a steady job as a lift engineer, on an entry-level rung of the ladder, but his job, unlike mine, was pretty secure and he earned around £17,000 a year with some night rate and overtime top-ups. In 2004, this seemed a princely sum to me.

In the weeks, months and years that followed, I turned my life from house share party animal to steadily and securely employed, housed mother of one. I felt for the first time in my life how much I was going to rely on politics. In my twenties, I could feel politics happening to me as a citizen. It was no longer something I was just going to debate down the pub with my mates. I could feel the people in the House of Commons changing my chances as if I was a character in a video game that they had to see safely past the treacherous platforms I could fall from and the cannonballs flying at me from all angles. I needed politics to get me to the end of the level.

In 2005, when our first son Harry was born, Tom and I didn't have much but we did have a secure tenancy in a home we could afford, and we would go on to buy our first home together two years later (almost unimaginable for a 25-year-old working part-time earning less than £12,000 per year). We both had jobs funded by our local council. Tom was working on the contract to fix the lifts in Birmingham's tower blocks and I was employed by local schemes for young offenders and vulnerable women, and also as a weekend respite carer for people with dementia and Alzheimer's.

We received Working Family tax credits and funding towards the cost of childcare so that I was able to go out to work and build up my experience for future work. Without this, I would almost certainly have not been able to work, as my husband's more secure job could not have been sacrificed, so mine would have been the thing to go.

My friends with kids and I had a local Sure Start centre we could visit for playgroups and breastfeeding support, or to check our baby's health and weight. The people that Tom and I met in those playgroups and stay-and-play schemes became our friends and support systems for the rest of our lives as parents.

Harry was given a free nursery place when he turned three years old and this felt like a lifeline from on high. It meant that I could work more hours and earn more money. The more hours and more money meant that by the time my second baby was born, Tom and I no longer relied on the state benefits that had been our lifeline when Harry was born.

Things were not always easy and they still aren't. We had huge amounts of help and support from our families and our friends. I still have the scars on my body and Tom and I have the lines on our faces to show that we worked hard and deserve a shed load of praise for the fact that our sons now have a level of security and financial privilege and advantage that we dreamed of. But it would be really wrong of me not to notice all the ways in which politics stopped me from tumbling off the various cliff edges that loomed in my life as I walked along the path.

Put aside the relatively clean, well-lit streets we both lived on growing up; put aside the universal education we both benefited from and the fact that neither of us has ever paid a penny every time we have been ill. Put aside that when one of our sons was born flat and blue with no breath in his lungs, we were lucky enough to be in a place where politics had provided free specialist staff to literally save his life and ours. Put aside the social housing my husband was born into that gave him warmth and shelter as a child. I am not even talking about all of these political decisions that were made before we were born that sought to give us, the citizens, a chance. I am talking about the politics I could actually feel happening to me as I became an active grown-up citizen.

In 2004, there were more women in the House of Commons than there ever had been before and, boy, as a woman citizen could I feel it. I could tell that the people who were now practising politics had struggled with childcare in their own lives and wanted to change it. I could tell that they had faced the horrible decision of whether they should give up work in order to look after their children because they couldn't afford to work on the lower wages paid to women and pay childcare. The tax credits I received every month into my account told me that someone, somewhere, knew how crappy it was that for some people, going to work does not pay the bills. Every time I applied for a job to support vulnerable people in my community through local charities, I could feel that someone, somewhere, was looking at their budget and thinking of ways to end the pain of many people in our society. When I set up savings accounts for my two sons, born to young, low-paid parents, with the money given to them by the government for when they turn eighteen, I knew that someone in an office in Whitehall had said, 'It is not fair that some kids have trust funds and others don't.' As a young mom, I could feel how Parliament was not perfect but that some of the people who gave their time to politics were a bit different – they might have lives like mine, they might have struggled with their kids and they understood my life.

My eldest son is sixteen now. He's about to leave school and go to college and he has the absolute audacity to think that at sixteen he can go to a school in London that specialises in film, his passion. My husband and I could not have conceived of such an idea when we were sixteen. We live minutes away from the homes we were born in. When I see that already my son has more choices than I did, I could weep at how grateful I am to the politics that my son was born into for not looking on me as a stupid girl who had got herself knocked up but instead saw me as a productive citizen who just needed some help to thrive and then reinvest in the country. The people in Parliament, especially the women in Parliament in the early 2000s, gave my son these choices. His success will be his own in the long run but his foundation came from the fact that there were people practicing politics who wanted young moms without a plan to be a success. I could mean it when I say I could cry at how grateful I feel for the chances I was given; I see it on the face of my son every single day.

Politics matters! Politics is not a game, it is not a toy for certain people to play with while others disengage. Politics is the reason that women have the vote, it is the reason that when you break your leg there is a place for you to go and get it fixed and if you are reading this in the UK, then the bill is on us. Politics is the reason that a man can no longer legitimately rape his wife in marriage. Politics is the universal education that exists in the great majority of the world. Politics is vaccination programmes that rid the world of smallpox, are close to ridding it of polio and are today helping to bring it back from the worst health crisis in many generations. Politics matters.

Politics is the thing that gave my nan and grandad a home to call their own after their streets were destroyed in the war.

And there is the rub, because politics started that war. Politics has killed many people through both active decisions and passive neglect. Politics tells one group of people to hate another. Politics provides a more ready platform for the richest in society than it does the common man. Politics gives power to people who then abuse it. Politics is horribly off-putting and for most people who have busy lives and have enough challenges to deal with, the downsides of politics are enough to make them disengage in despair. Who could blame them?

Politics is not perfect, not even close. In my time on the political front line, I have seen so much that is wrong. I have seen how the language and traditions of our Parliament actively make people feel excluded from joining in: 'I could never do what you do because I don't know all the language.' My hope for this book is that in letting people behind the curtain a little bit, they can see that many of us who work in politics once upon a time didn't know the language. And there are lots of us who play almost no bloody attention to the language we are supposed to use and, as much as possible, try to make Parliament into a more modern place.

I have seen how politics can corrupt genuinely good intentions. The terrifying spotlight that accompanies it can stop people from being courageous; it allows the whole political class to be painted as lemmings who will agree to anything. I have watched Cabinet ministers having to sell an idea I know perfectly well from chats with them in the tearoom that they think is absolutely batshit, only to have to distance themselves from it a few days later because their political leadership has changed their mind. That makes politicians look like spineless, useless fools. I would like to start a revolution of people answering the bloody question they are asked and when they have got something wrong saying so. 'Yep, I was wrong last week because we are all wrong from time to time and it's much better if we can admit this and then work on improving it.' We would be pilloried for the first few weeks but the public at home would like it much more than the people who write the column inches. What happens now is that everyone knows a politician has done something wrong and yet we have to watch them tangling themselves in knots, saying ridiculous things on national telly like, 'Of course we all drive our children around to test our eyesight,' trying to avoid just saying that politics is really bloody complicated and there is no such thing as perfect.

We have not done anywhere near enough to make politics about the people it is meant to serve, by being brave enough to treat them like adults who can very well understand that life is not always easy and sometimes they won't be happy. Politics has made a very poor attempt at inviting people to understand and respect the complexities of our legislature and the legislation it churns out. Over all of my political career for the past decade, I have watched as a politics that talks about people's hope for the future and then actually delivers it has given way to quick, hopeful slogans that are basically just lies. I have watched while, instead of admitting that it got things wrong and could have done better, the political class looked around for a convenient bogeyman to blame for the pain its citizens are feeling: immigrants, the EU, people on benefits for one side; bankers, the richest and business for the other. I honestly could scream because the truth of it is that these scapegoats of whichever flavour just get in the way of us rolling up our sleeves and just bloody well getting on with trying to improve things. When did we get to this age of politics getting in the way of common sense?

Politics that actually works engages its citizens and makes them feel that they can reach out to their representative, get help and advice, and give help and advice in equal measure. Politics that works would create a news cycle that gives more column inches to the policies of politicians than it does to a newscaster laughing at the size of the flag in the background of a press conference.

The game of politics and who gets the most likes or incites the most anger is a tiny fraction of the work that happens in the Palace of Westminster every day. Day in, day out, there is someone squirrelled away in an office that is crumbling around their ears, in some cases with the toilets on the floor above leaking onto their desks, trying to find a council flat for an elderly woman who has had a fall and can't manage the stairs in the house she has lived in for fifty years. That same person is then working with their teams to draft new laws that would help elderly people downsize to more suitable sheltered and caring accommodation so that in the future this individual's battle will be less hard. Later that day, that same politician might make a gaffe on a TV show and not know the price of milk* and that will be the

---

* Seriously, anyone who ever tries to shrink down the experiences of 99 per cent of the citizens of this country by asking for the price of bread and milk also thinks that all northerners race whippets and wear cloth caps. Ordinary people do not obsess about knowing the price of bread and milk; I have literally never had a conversation with anyone about the price of bread and milk, although I do have a WhatsApp group about the latest crazy brilliant things that are available in the central aisle of Lidl.

thing he or she will be remembered for. It will likely make it into their obituary.

Politics, how it's practised and the people doing it do leave a lot to be desired at times. Just like you and me, they make mistakes and get things wrong. The trouble is when they get stuff wrong people can die and our country can be put in danger. We are right to expect more from them and demand that they act like servants of the people. I am happy to serve; I am less happy to be enslaved by fear and cynicism.

I totally understand why ordinary citizens disengage from politics in despair, but please know that every day that they do we leave the pitch completely clear for the same people who have always held the power, who all went to the same school and who I very much doubt ever had to think about if they would need to give up their job to look after the kids.

It is on all of us to stop treating politics like a game or a gameshow. It is on all of us to engage so that we don't keep churning out prime ministers who all went to the same school. We are not merely spectators of a soap opera or a racy big-budget drama – this is all of our lives. It is on us all to find out much more about what is going in that crumbly palace and its counterparts around the world. I went into frontline politics for all sorts of reasons and, as I said when we started this journey together, it was because I had a notion that politics could change the world for the better, because I had seen it in my own life that if more people like me had their bums on the seats in the local council chamber, in the offices in Westminster and Whitehall, in the seats at the United Nations and in the meeting rooms of embassies around the world, then the politics that came out the other end was more likely to serve people like me and my son.

I dedicated this book to my brother Luke. He might not be a young man but he is a man finishing university and, just like me, he has two young sons. He also has unstable tenancy and inappropriate housing for his family. My brother and his children need politics to give them a chance just like it gave me and my son a chance to be safe and well. My brother needs politics to see him. And so he turns up to meetings, he writes to his MP, he learns about the processes involved and he takes part in those processes to make it happen. Politics is not something that happens in a fancy building. Politics is ours: never let someone who doesn't sound like you, who wouldn't dream of going to the same school as you, who thinks they can just throw you a slogan without ever actually planning on delivering it make you feel as if politics is for someone else. It's ours and it only gets better when we make it better.

Thanks for reading about the weirdness of the place where I work, thanks for caring about politics and what is right and wrong about it. You don't have to end up an MP to take part – simply wanting to find out what political life is like is an act of resistance against the idea that politics happens in a golden palace where you are not welcome.

That palace belongs to you.

Glossary of Terms

adjournment debate

This is a debate that takes place after Parliament has finished its normal business for the day and the House has adjourned. There is an adjournment debate every day and it can be about anything an MP wants to discuss. It is not voted on but is a way to raise an issue and have a minister listen and give you a public response, which you can then hold them to.

All–Party Parliamentary Group (APPG)

All–Party Parliamentary Groups (APPGs) are groupings of cross-party members of the House of Commons and the House of Lords that focus on a specific issue. They will run regular evidence meetings with experts (experts by experience as well as those with specific professional qualifications) and produce reports and recommendations to lobby the government on their particular issue. There is an APPG for every country in the world – the China APPG, the India APPG, etc. – which arrange trips to foster relations with these countries. In fact, there has been an APPG for pretty much everything, including vintage cars and calligraphy – although

I'm not sure they have to do much lobbying when it comes to calligraphy, as from what I can tell it is alive and well in the Commons.

backbencher

A backbench MP is someone who has no allocated job or role within their political party. If you are a government minister, or in opposition a shadow minister, you are considered a frontbench MP because you are entitled to sit in the front row in the chamber of the House of Commons and speak from the despatch box (the two fancy wooden boxes in the centre you see ministers delivering speeches from on TV). Most MPs are backbenchers. 'Backbencher' is also used to refer to an MP who is more free to express their opinion, who is a bit of a maverick or a renegade – but, I hasten to add, not in any exciting sense, just that they occasionally question the actions of their own party. That's about as risky as it gets.

the campaign

In election law in the UK, there are two periods in the lead up to an election known as the long and short campaigns. There are regulations determining how much money you can spend and what you can and can't say and do in these periods. The long and short campaign timeframe and financial restrictions are decided by the electoral commission in the UK and monitored and regulated by them. Personally I am not sure how strongly this regulation is enforced, as people seem to get away with all sorts.

The long campaign: this period can start anywhere up to six months before an election, once the election date is fixed. It usually lasts around twelve weeks, prior to the short campaign kicking off.

The short campaign: this begins from the moment that Parliament is dissolved in anticipation of an election, usually six to eight weeks before the election happens. At this point, all seats in the House of Commons become vacant. We are no longer MPs, we are now simply candidates for the position and are considered legally to have exactly the same rights as any other candidate who is standing against us. During this period, I am not allowed to refer to myself as Jess Phillips MP; I am not allowed to use the fancy headed paper that has the symbols of Parliament on. The sign above the door of my office in Birmingham that says 'Jess Phillips MP' has to be covered up. During this time the rent on my office is not paid for by Parliament; I pay it so that I can use it to campaign from, which would not otherwise be allowed. It is a very weird period, not least because my constituents still come to me for help as usual, but I am just helping them as Jess Phillips and not as an MP. My staff who work for Parliament, not the Labour Party, can carry on their work but any time that they spend on the election must be their own.

casework

MPs' casework breaks down into two distinct parts. Constituency casework includes all of the requests for help and advice on anything – and I really mean anything – that we receive from our constituents. Policy casework is the correspondence that we get from our constituents about their views on national policy, most of which is driven to us from campaign petition sites and is not personal to the constituent but tells us what their beliefs are. Both have to be responded to and followed up.

civil servant

Civil servants are people who work for government departments and report to ministers. They are not meant to act politically and for the most part this is adhered to. Civil servants make up the teams of people who are employed to help advise the government on policy and do the actual work of enacting the government's decisions. They are the people who do the nuts-and-bolts work of governance, from staffing your local job centre to advising prime ministers on war. In the chamber of the House of Commons, there is a bench behind the Speaker's chair where senior civil servants sit so that when ministers are in debates, giving statements to the House of Commons or being asked questions, the civil servants can pass them notes with useful information.

constituency / constituent

My constituency is the area that I represent and my constituents are all the people who live in it. Constituents and electors are different in that many of my constituents are not electors because they cannot or do not wish to be registered to vote. Of these, most cannot register because they are under eighteen while others are not British or Commonwealth citizens. In my constituency of Yardley, that is a lot of people. I have thousands and thousands of constituents who cannot and will not ever vote for me but I still serve them exactly as I do the electors.

the division bell

In the Palace of Westminster, bells are used like they are at school (in fact, many aspects of Parliament are reminiscent of some sort of public school in a children's book). In every corridor and office in Westminster, there is a speaker that blares out the sound of bells when the parliamentary session starts each day and when it finishes. The division bell is also used to alert MPs that there is a vote taking place and will ring for eight minutes to summon us to make our way to the chamber of the House of Commons in order to vote. In these modern times we also receive a text from our political parties, but the bells still ring. The term 'division' came about because MPs have not yet found a way to agree – they are divided and so 'division' becomes the stand-in word for a vote. Really it just means 'the vote bell'.

Early Day Motion

An Early Day Motion is just an expression of interest that is committed to the public record and MPs can put their names to it. EDMs are often issue-based or an act of congratulating or commiserating. 'That this House notes with sadness the passing of Dundee United legend Jim McLean, the team's most successful manager' is an example from the day I wrote this. They don't change anything, they are just a public expression of interest that members of Parliament can sign up to.

exit poll

An election exit poll is a survey of voters taken immediately after they have left the polling stations having cast their votes. Academics and private companies working for newspapers or broadcasters conduct exit polls to gain an early indication as to how an election has turned out, as in many elections the actual result may take hours. In the 2020 US election, for example, it took days to count the votes. The exit poll is pretty accurate compared to other opinion polls, which ask people to imagine how they might feel on an election day in the future, because it is sampling how people actually did vote rather than how they might, hypothetically.

the expenses scandal

The expenses scandal was a major political scandal originally uncovered in 2009 by the *Telegraph* newspaper. It concerned expenses claims made by members of Parliament and members of the House of Lords and brought to light widespread misuse of allowances and expenses permitted to members of Parliament. The public was rightly appalled and it resulted in a large number of resignations, sackings and retirements of MPs. Many had to give public apologies and repay the money they had claimed. Several members or former members of both the House of Commons and the House of Lords were prosecuted and sent to prison. I entered Parliament six years after all this had come to light and the entire expenses regime had been completely changed.

hustings

A hustings is a meeting usually organised by a local group, such as a residents association or school, where all of the election candidates in an area are invited to come and present themselves. It is like the leaders debates on telly, but in a draughty church hall or library. The usual format is for each candidate to introduce themselves for three minutes or so, after which the public pose questions that every candidate has to answer in turn.

Ipsos MORI

Ipsos MORI is a market research company that undertakes political polling (asking a sample of the British public their opinion) on policy and how people will vote. A lot of politics is driven by the results of polls from these companies and yet I am still to actually meet anyone in the wild who has ever been polled by one of these companies; it's on my bucket list.

the Leader of the House of Commons

The Leader of the House of Commons is not really the leader of anything: they are the person in government who manages the business of what happens in the building of Westminster and, along with the Speaker of the Commons, is responsible for the state of the building and enforcing its rules.

lobby

Lobby means many things in Parliament.

To lobby (v.) means to meet, discuss and pressure someone to your way of thinking. I lobby government ministers to do what I want and, in turn, I am lobbied by constituents to do what they want. There are people whose job is to lobby for companies and charities professionally, and they are called lobbyists.

The lobby (n.) is also the collective noun we use for the journalists who work in Parliament. If you are a journalist who is based in the building, rather than one who watches from afar, and your job is to write stories about us, then you are a lobby correspondent. Lobby correspondents all sit in the gallery above the chamber of the House of Commons writing up what they hear and see, or they are to be found hanging around in Westminster, chatting in corridors.

Then there are the various spaces in Parliament referred to as a lobby, such as the Central Lobby, which is where constituents have a right to come and appeal for an audience to lobby their member of Parliament (although these days most use email). There is the Members' Lobby, which is where MPs loiter when we are waiting for a vote and where we lobby each other to sign up to campaigns or ask for people to join in with our debates, etc. And the lobby is also the name for the two corridors either side of the chamber of the House of Commons where we vote. There is a No Lobby and an Aye (yes) Lobby; we vote by walking through these lobbies and saying our names to the clerks sat at the end.

In Parliament, we make the word 'lobby' work very hard.

marginal seat

A seat where the result in the previous election was close between the top two candidates. You also get seats where there is not much between the top three candidates, which we call three-way marginals. I don't think there is any official number that is used to define a marginal seat but I would say anything less than a majority of 5,000 would be considered marginal.

Marginal seats tend to see a lot of political activity and campaigning. In safer seats where the previous winning candidate (the current MP) had a majority over 10,000, there is less likelihood that the seat will change hands between political parties and the election is therefore less hotly contested. Mind you, there seems to be no such thing as a safe seat anymore and recently, seats that were always Labour have now turned Conservative and vice versa.

the Palace of Westminster and associated buildings

The Palace of Westminster is the name for the 'old bit' of the parliamentary estate, which is famous the world over. It includes the chamber of the House of Commons (the room you see on TV in debates and PMQs with all the green benches), the House of Lords and, most famously, Big Ben.

The House of Commons is both an institution and a building. The House of Commons (institution) refers to elected members of Parliament – i.e., commoners not fancy lords. The Commons is the name for the chamber of the House of Commons and all the offices, libraries, committee rooms, etc., used by MPs.

The Lords, or House of Lords, is the unelected chamber of the Houses of Parliament for hereditary and life peers. Lady lords are called baronesses but obviously we still call the building the Lords because, well . . . sexism. The chamber of the House of Lords doesn't make it on to TV as much as the

Commons but is basically the same but with red benches, more gold fittings and a posher carpet.

There are lots of rooms within the House of Parliament where lords and commoners mix, various tearooms and bars etc., but as a rule, elected members of the Commons go to the Commons library and tearooms and the Lords to theirs.

Portcullis House, or PCH, is the newer part of the Westminster complex. This office building was built in 1992 to give MPs more meeting rooms, private offices and a big atrium to act as a general meeting space. It is where most MPs have their offices and it links to other parts of the estate such as the Norman Shaw Building and 1 Parliament Street, which also house MPs' offices.

Prime Minister's Questions (PMQs)

PMQs is the top-billed event in Parliament. It happens every Wednesday at noon sharp and, as advertised, it is half an hour for members of Parliament to put questions to the prime minister.

the returning officer

The returning officer is the official in charge of the logistics that ensure an election happens. They organise all of the polling stations and make sure they are staffed securely; they are responsible for making sure the election candidates behave properly and they make sure of all the legal necessities of the election, the candidates and the count. The returning officer is usually a senior officer in the local authority or local council.

Speaker of the House

There is a Speaker of the House of Commons and a Speaker of the House of Lords, each fulfilling the same role in the two different chambers. The job of the Speaker is to manage all of the business of the chamber. As the chair they call out the instructions and make sure the proceedings keep to time, are within the rules and are polite and cordial. Obviously this last bit is the hardest, and when MPs get rowdy and shouty with each other the Speaker will shout 'Order', will pick out the badly behaved and can dole out punishments if people do not immediately apologise for their poor behaviour or rule-breaking. The Speaker can eject members of parliament from the building and dock their pay for the number of days for which they remain excluded.

This is the public face of the Speaker; behind the scenes they also fulfil a managerial role with regards to the building and the people who work there. The speaker oversees many decisions involving security, the building and the rules and regulations of how Parliament will work. It is a massive job.

target seat

Each political party will draw up a list of seats that it has determined it has a chance of winning and so will be prioritised during an election campaign when it comes to funding and resources. Target seats can be ones that the party already has and wants to hold against a strong threat – called defensive targets – but usually they are the ones held by your opponent that you think you can win.

an urgent question

This is the definition on the UK Parliament website: 'If an urgent or important matter arises which an MP believes requires an immediate answer from a government minister, they may apply to ask an urgent question. MPs may request that the Speaker considers their application for an Urgent Question each day.'

However, an urgent question is not just one question, as the above would imply, it is one topic. So, for example, you might have asked for an urgent question to be put to the Secretary of State for Housing the day after the Grenfell Tower disaster. What that means is that the Secretary of State has to come to the Commons, or delegate this to their junior ministers, and answer the initial question, at which point other MPs can ask questions on the same topic. Essentially, an urgent question is an hour-long grilling for a government minister on the important issues of the day.

whip (or 'party whip')

As with 'lobby', the whip means more than one thing – but in this instance none of them are what you might think. It is not a whip like Indiana Jones has. There is no one in Parliament whose job it is to literally flay MPs.

Like all things in Parliament, the term 'whip' is rooted in an old posh tradition that bears absolutely no relation to modern politics, or the modern world. This is one of the hazards of an institution set up by and largely populated by a load of posh blokes: lots of the words that we still use today relate to things these posh blokes did hundreds of years ago.

If you listen to MPs speaking in Parliament, they say things like, 'I wish to address the Honourable Gentleman', which obviously sounds really stupid and isn't how anyone actually talks to each other today. In Parliament, traditions die hard.

The 'whip' comes from language used in hunting, that super modern and popular sport of the masses. I have never been on a hunt and I never intend to go on a hunt, which is lucky as I am not sure there are many fox hunts in inner-city Birmingham – although there are loads of foxes. But apparently, on a hunt there is the 'whipper-in' who keeps the 'hounds' (what most people would call 'dogs') together in a pack by whipping them (this time with an actual whip).

So what is it in Parliament? It is actually the term for three things. They are:

- *The whip (person): a member of Parliament who is picked by the political party leaders to make MPs vote for things that that political party wants. So I guess the Whip is the huntsman, and presumably that makes me, as an MP, one of the hounds.*
- *The whip (document): the instruction that is sent around weekly to say what will be happening in the House of Commons the following week. I can frequently be heard asking other MPs, 'What's the whip on Monday?' so I know if I need to be in Parliament or not. This is where the term 'three-line whip' comes from, because on the document, the details of that day would literally be underlined three times.*
- *The whip (instruction): the term is also used to refer to the actual instruction from your party leaders on how you are meant to vote on each individual vote.*

So the whip is a person, a document and an instruction. Posh men may have loved a hunt, but turns out they were less good on coming up with names for things. The most common use of the term, though, is to describe the person. Each political party selects a team of whips. There is one Chief Whip, two Deputy Chief Whips and then a team of ordinary whips below them. The number of whips each party has depends on the size of the political party. The Green Party, for example, have only ever had one MP in Parliament, so they obviously don't have a team of whips. Parties with fewer than twenty MPs would usually only have one whip, whereas the Conservative and Labour parties tend to have around fifteen whips.

Acknowledgements

This is my absolutely favourite bit of book writing; the acknowledgements. I write this usually halfway through writing the first chapter of the book as I find it inspires me to keep going. Also, it is a brilliant way to procrastinate when all the washing is done and I've cleaned all my make-up brushes, which I only ever do when I am writing a book.

I want to thank Holly Harris and Kat Ailes and all of the team at Simon & Schuster. I signed this deal in the middle of a global pandemic and only met them on Zoom when they decided to take a punt on me. They have been brilliant throughout. Holly perfectly manages the balancing act of encouraging me with praise at the same time as not letting me off the hook. It is very easy to make excuses when you are a frontline politician in the middle of a global pandemic.

To my brilliant agent and friend Laura Macdougall, who gave birth to the beautiful Thea in the middle of this book being written. I simply do not possess the faith in myself that she seems to have in me and for which I am eternally grateful. Laura, you will be the best of mums to Thea, I am in awe of your resilience! To Olivia Davies from United Agents, who took on the unenviable task of working with me while Laura was on maternity leave, you have been great.

This is a book about politics and I hope that it has given people more faith in – or at least understanding of – the system of democracy in our country. When I started in the big house at SW1A I knew very little, and I would not have ever reached the platform that I have today without my colleagues supporting and guiding me. I would not remain sane in Westminster without my colleagues and friends; I won't list them because I fear I might miss someone out and then there will be some kind of political schism. But they know who they are; they are the ones who make me laugh. To the likes of Margaret Hodge, Harriet Harman, Rosie Winterton, Yvette Cooper and David Lammy, who have always been supportive elder statespeople to whom I could turn in desperation when I have no idea what is going on or what I should do next. They are the kind of people who push other people forward rather than grabbing the mic, and in politics this is bloody rare.

Special thanks must absolutely go to Chris Bryant, who fits into most of the categories above. He keeps me going and he is an elder statesman but I put him in a category all of his own because he knows so bloody much about the history and procedure of Parliament; I have essentially delegated all of my understanding of the complicated procedures of the Commons to him. Between him and the Labour whips office I have been able to clear headspace for the things I care about while they are clever enough to both understand the procedure and simultaneously care about stuff.

To those who lost their seats due to a period of political

idiocy within my party, a special thanks goes to Anna Turley, Ruth Smeeth, Gareth Snell, Melanie Onn and Phil Wilson, who definitely all still keep me going in politics regardless of the fact that it must be pretty painful for them to keep going.

I learned most of what I know about campaigning from Caroline Badley; she remains my political lodestar. And to all of my very keen staff, past and present, thanks for making me look good and as if I am in more than one place at a time.

To Tom, Harry and Danny, who don't give a toss about political life but are forced to live it, thanks as always. To my girlfriends who bring me down a peg or two when I get a bit big for my boots, thanks for helping me to not think about politics from time to time, with special mention to Amy Eddy who, when I went on *Question Time*, asked me if I'd won because she thought I had appeared on *Mastermind*. Thanks for keeping me real.

I dedicated this book to my brother Luke because while I was writing it Luke got a first class honours degree in Political Science from Birmingham University. He started his degree while still addicted to heroin and cocaine; he is now clean and sober, and working to make the world a better place. As I mentioned, but it bears repeating, he once told me, 'I study politics. That's different to what you do; I actually know what I am talking about.'

And, as I hope I have made clear, politics is for everyone, so a final thanks to you, the reader, for picking up this book and deciding to take part.